Baltimore: Persons and Places

Mark N. Ozer

DEDICATED TO MY BALTIMORE FRIENDS

TABLE OF CONTENTS

ACKNOWLEGEMENTS

Thanks particularly to Francis O'Neil of the Maryland Historical Society Library for his thoughtful review of the manuscript. To Deborah Wiener Research Historian and Family Life Coordinator Jewish Museum of Maryland/Jeffrey Korman Director of the Maryland Room at the Enoch Pratt Central Library, Paul Espinosa Librarian Peabody Institute and the Reference Service of the Library of Congress and the Bender Library at the American University. To all my friends who helped me in my exploration of Baltimore: Carol Warner, Vincent Tobin, Gilbert Sandler, Catherine Frick Beyer, Kathy Ozer, David Battey, Marianne Levin and Leon Levin, Susan and Philip Abraham, Brigitte and Nicholas Fessenden, George Thompson, and Eduard Berlin.

INTRODUCTION

The Chesapeake Bay is actually the Valley of the Susquehanna River drowned by the rise in sea level after the end of the Ice Age. The bay's name is a corruption of the local Algonquin speakers' word for "Great Water." Rivers from the Susquehanna south to the York and James including the Potomac, the Patuxent, the Piscataway and the Patapsco form the largest estuary in the United States.

The earliest European settlers entered the Chesapeake Bay in 1607 between Cape Henry, named after the elder son of James I, and Cape Charles named after his second son, to settle at Jamestown on the James River. Captain John Smith explored the area from 1607 to 1609 and published his map in 1612. The country was inhabited by the peaceful Piscataway tribe subject to the warlike more northerly Iroquoian-speaking Susquehannocks. Both tribes eventually succumbed to the depredations of war, disease and civilization. What came to be called the Patapsco (meaning "backwater") River in the Algonquin tongue was identified by John Smith after its red iron bearing soil as "Bolus flu." Appearing as merely an estuary of the bay, it is actually a river extending some fifty miles inland.

The estuary of the Patapsco River is broader and deeper and extends farther inland than the smaller rivers that flow into the Chesapeake that had been the site of previous towns such as Annapolis, based on the tobacco trade derived from southern Maryland. The mouth of the Patapsco River is the "basin" on the western shore of the Chesapeake Bay that became the harbor of

Baltimore. The present-day Baltimore Harbor Tunnel, eight miles upriver from its mouth, is the narrowest portion of the basin and divides the "bay portion" of the basin from the "harbor portion." The latter, extending to the edge of what became the site of the town, consists of the Northwest Branch (Inner Harbor from Fort McHenry at Whetstone Point to Calvert Street) and the Middle Branch.

Emptying into the Middle Branch, one can follow the Main Branch up as it continues to Elkridge Landing, once the site of a Colonial seaport at the head of navigation. That area also had an early iron forge and furnace using local surface deposits of limestone and iron ore. Continuing 6 miles further up, the river flows in a rocky canyon past Ellicott City with, from 1774 onward, its extensive "Patapsco Flour" mills; then past the Falls of the Patapsco to its origin. The last is a pool called Parr Spring in the piedmont at the intersection of the boundaries of Carroll, Howard, Frederick and Montgomery Counties in central Maryland. This highest point is on a ridge is 800-1000 feet from the coastal plain at the Fall Line just above Elkridge to reach sea level at the harbor.

The sandy soil of the tidewater area was the site of early settlement in both Maryland and Virginia. The method used for tobacco cultivation depleted the virgin land; created an agricultural economy that required continual expansion into areas further north and west as well as intensive labor increasingly performed by enslaved Africans. Starting in the 1730s, many small settlements arose at several sites in the western area drained by the Chesapeake Bay. These several towns, one of which was Baltimore, arose where tobacco, brought down from the local plantations, could be loaded for transport to England.

During the French and Indian War, the depredations carried out by the Indians after the defeat of General Braddock at Fort Duquesne in 1755 are credited with the early growth of Baltimore. The safety of the port made it more attractive to arriving settlers than places further west threatened by Indian attacks. A further influx of inhabitants occurred with the expulsion of the Acadian French from Nova Scotia by the British conquest of Canada in 1763 that formed one of the earliest Catholic congregations. Until then, unlike the plantations of the Eastern Shore, Baltimore had been a mainly Protestant town.

By the 1750s, with the economy more dependent upon the export of grain being raised in western Maryland and ironworking, towns such as Baltimore along the Fall Line became even more prominent. Situated where the heavier clayey soils of the Piedmont meet the lighter sandy soils of the Tidewater, the topography of Baltimore with hills and watercourses has controlled its development and its subsequent street system. Its geography has been its destiny.

The towns that similarly arose even further west bordering the Potomac River in the 1740s such as Georgetown and Alexandria became incorporated after the 1790s within the District of Columbia. Their commercial focus, at first paramount, eventually became superseded by their role as components of the national capital. The fate of the town of Baltimore differed with its superior deep harbor that arose as a port on the Northwest Branch of the Patapsco.

Illustrative of the difference in focus was the capitalization of banks in the 1790s. The total of $6 million in Baltimore chartered by the State of Maryland was twice that of banks in the District of Columbia. In the 1830s when the population of the City of Washington reached 20,000 and growing only very slowly, that of Baltimore had reached 80,000 and would grow rapidly during the next few decades. By 1850, Baltimore had become second only to New York, edging out Philadelphia. Unlike the settlements on the Potomac joining the District of Columbia, Baltimore remained within the State of Maryland to become a great American city based upon its better port and more effective connection to the growing west.

The early fortune of Baltimore was founded on its presence on the fall line. In the days of water power, Jones Falls, complemented by Gwynns Falls and Herring Run, had far more substantial flow than the comparable Rock Creek in the District of Columbia and from a greater height. Industry clung to its shores more tenaciously and remained even when the mills became larger and steam driven. Moreover, the harbor was far better, without sandbars and shoals, particularly when extended to the east at Fells Point and later yet to the south. The access to the interior was superior in the days of waterborne transport and then through the National Road and particularly via the Baltimore & Ohio Railroad.

Ultimately even more important was the character of the people who settled there. Immigration from the north from Pennsylvania and then from Europe, particularly Germany, brought a hard working relatively skilled population that was continually replenished by other immigrants into what was after all a Southern city. By 1840, the city was one-fifth German. They and others built a commercial city that in turn built the railroads that enhanced its development further as also an industrial city. A place built on business, its physical development was the fruit of speculative building superimposed upon the somewhat reluctant hilly topography. The street system, initially mainly connecting the settled area east to west along the shoreline of the harbor, successively entered onto the hills to the north and west as well as the more accessible less hilly east. An upper class divided by diversity of religion failed to generate a city-wide vision. Segregation based on class, ethnicity and race coupled with large scale immigration of both whites and blacks has created the character of the city as well as limiting its progress and perhaps its ultimate success.

The fruit of persons who imposed their will on its geography, Baltimore in its history was also the source of several important ideas that contributed to the rest of the United States. One was the idea of the separation of government and religion. First expressed by the founding family in the 17th century, it provided the basis for the initial growth of the American Catholic Church as a minority religion in a form different from its evolution elsewhere in the world. A second major contribution was the development of the first railroad to connect the farmlands of the west to the port cities. This connection profoundly changed the evolution of the entire country, eventually creating an east-west unity that prevailed in the Civil War. Still another was the concept of the graduate university and the introduction of science into the practice of medicine and medical education. The ongoing civil rights revolution of the 20th century also had many of its roots in Baltimore. More local in its impact have been its great philanthropists, several actually originally from New England, who created the cultural institutions that have made Baltimore a great city in its own right.

Successive chapters follow the development of the city over the nearly 300 years since its founding in 1729. Significant breakpoints are the Battle of Baltimore at the end of the War of 1812, the Civil War when Baltimore was split as a focal point after its growth as a commercial city to be the third largest in the United States; its industrial growth along with the industrialization of America but in an era when Baltimore no longer maintained its rate of growth and was faced by the Great Fire of 1904. Despite the impetus given by the rapid recovery from that devastating fire, subsequent chapters in the 20th century mark an even greater failure to thrive and its ultimate de-industrialization while still suffering the legacy of divisiveness, segregation and poor schooling for the underclass. As it entered the 21st century, the transition to a service economy has been hailed as the "Baltimore Renaissance." Yet, like so many other American cities, its legacy of environmental degradation and mean spiritness cannot be easily overcome. Long delayed and still incomplete, the development of a rapid transit system uniting the various segments of the city and region holds promise for the future as does its outstanding universities and medical facilities.

At each stage, we explore the role of salient persons who have contributed not only to that development but may have had a wider impact. In each chapter, this book couples the development of the economy and politics, streets, buildings and the monuments of the city, the *place* with some of the *persons* whose impact can still be seen on that place.

CHAPTER 1
THE BALTIMORE TOWN
1729-1815

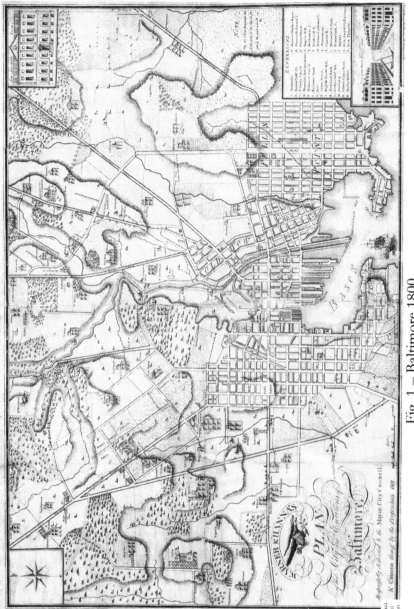

Fig. 1 – Baltimore 1800

14

1.1 The Early Port/To Mt Vernon Place

Baltimore County was laid out in 1659 on the western shore of Chesapeake Bay along with Calvert and Anne Arundel Counties in addition to the original St Mary's County. When first laid out in 1659, Baltimore County included all of present day Cecil (1673), Harford (1773) and Carroll (1837) Counties and portions of Anne Arundel, Howard and Frederick Counties (from Patapsco on the west to Chester River on the Eastern Shore). Hillier than its sister counties, its terrain discouraged the initial settlers looking for large tracts of easily exploited plain for tobacco cultivation.

Herring Run rises in Towson to run through the eastern portion of the county where it defines the Fall Line of the Back River between the Piedmont and the Coastal Plain. The birthplace of America's iron industry in the 18th century, the British-owned Principio Company's overcutting of the watershed's tree cover caused the Run to silt over leading to the ultimate destruction of the industry dependent on its flow for power. During the colonial era, Maryland was the largest producer of iron despite competition from New York and Pennsylvania.

The ownership by the Principio Company of extensive tracts of land precluded other development in this area. The confiscation of its property during the American Revolution led to the division of the land into country estates for the merchant elite and truck farms that lasted until late into the 19th century.

The original Baltimore town in 1729 lay alongside the Northwest Branch harbor basin (Inner Harbor) whose shallow depth was originally adequate to serve the sailing ships of the time. Entering into the Northwest Branch were the two other streams that further define the town that arose. Their names also signify their proquinity to the Fall Line in which Baltimore lies. Jones Falls runs along Falls Road to help form the reservoir at Lake Roland, enters a gorge with banks sufficient for mills in Hampden-Woodberry before emptying into the harbor basin just to the east; while Gwynns Falls rising near Pikesville rushing down near Dickeyville and Forest Park empties into the Middle Branch of the Patapsco near the post established in the 17th century by Richard Gwinn for trade with the Indians at the ford at its mouth. Nearby was the iron mine owned by John Moale that led him to oppose the settlement of a town at that site; and later still were the iron mills owned by the Carroll family to the west using Gwynns Falls.

The streets of the original modest sixty acre parcel bought from the Carroll family were laid out on the small area of flat land abutting the Northwest Branch. Unlike the grand plan of Washington, the town was laid out using the otherwise commonly prevailing grid street pattern patterned after that of neighboring Philadelphia. However, unlike that city, there were no redeeming green squares to relieve the grid. The north-south streets were bound by Jones's Falls with marsh alongside on the north and east and a gully to the northwest. It ran from present-day Saratoga Street on the north to Halliday Street on the east. Some street names still recall their colonial origins reminiscent of London such as Lombard Street that faced the water as well as the German origins of the Georgian kings in Hanover Street and Brunswick Street.

Chartered in 1732, the area to the east of Jones's Falls known as Jones's Town was merged as "Old Town" in 1745. This area is bound by Pratt and Monument Streets immediately to the east of Jones Falls through which ran the York, Harford, Belair and the Philadelphia Roads in their various directions. The shipbuilding area of Fell's Point laid out in the 1730s still farther to the east with its far deeper harbor was annexed in 1773. Baltimore was thus from the start an amalgamation of several separate entities with their somewhat different street patterns that limited the sense of amalgamation.

Gay Street, named after Nicholas Ruxton Gay who helped lay out the town, was the first street carrying a bridge across Jones Falls to Jones's Town to the east. The latter's twenty acres of streets were laid out in a rectangle wherein the streets followed the meander of the falls separated by a twenty-eight acre marsh. The marsh land bordering Jones Falls dividing the original town from the Jones's Town was bought by Thomas Harrison and filled in leading to the joining of the two settlements but not necessarily the street names or their street lines.

Fell's Point in turn farther east continues to reflect its maritime and colonial origin in Thames Street. Its streets are also laid out in the usual grid aside from the Point where the streets followed the lay of the land. To encourage development the land was sold with no money down but ground rent would be paid, confirming the financing mechanism already established by Thomas Harrison in selling lots in the former marsh. This pattern was to prevail in Baltimore: less capital was required for building since no payment was necessary for the underlying land. The buyer was assured of longevity since the 99 year leases were renewable; the seller was assured a safe passive investment that would increase in value as improvements would be made by the tenants.

After the 1750s, the original trade in tobacco to England that had preferred Annapolis expanded to include trade to the sugar plantations in the West Indies. Rather than tobacco, flour would be the major export and now from the port of Baltimore milled by water power from grain raised in adjacent areas of Pennsylvania and western Maryland. The grain shipments encouraged the development of grist mills on the Jones Falls, Gwynns Falls and at the Ellicott Mills at the Falls of the Patapsco. The flour was easier to ship and would last longer in the hot climate of the West Indies than that milled in the cool damp climate of still farther away England.

The names of several important streets still reflect the founding family. The major east-west street (Market Street) was given the name of the Lords Baltimore and the major north-south street that of their Calvert family name. Although these two streets formed the first important crossroad, the meeting of Baltimore and Charles Streets became the actual center of the street numbering system of the entire city when that system was established in 1886. All streets are thus delineated as north or south of Baltimore and east or west of Charles

Streets. The accompanying map shows Baltimore in 1800 incorporating the original town with adjoining Jones Town and Fells Point surrounding the Inner Harbor.

1.2. The Lords Baltimore and the "Maryland Design"

George Calvert was the name of the 1st Lord Baltimore, the Proprietor of the colony of Maryland. Born on the family estate in strongly Catholic Yorkshire, he was raised as a hidden Catholic forced to swear public conformity to the Protestant faith. The religious settlement of 1559 after the accession of Queen Elizabeth I equated loyalty to the English state to adherence to the national church. Adherence to the Catholic religion inferred loyalty to the Pope, a foreign prince, and made one subject to severe penalties, tempered by these laws' only intermittent enforcement.

Fig 2 – George Calvert, 1st Lord Baltimore

19

George Calvert graduated from Oxford's Trinity College in 1597 and studied law at Lincoln's Inn. While travelling on the continent, he met Sir Robert Cecil when the latter was on a mission to the court of Henry of Navarre (later Henry IV of France). Calvert rose to power and wealth as the protégé of Secretary of State Cecil following the accession of James VI of Scotland to the English throne as James I. Even after the death of Cecil, Calvert continued to advance in favor. One mark of favor was election to a seat in Parliament; another was clerk and then Secretary to the Privy Council and a knighthood. After resigning his office of Secretary in 1625 mainly because of internal court politics in relation to support of a Spanish marriage for the heir, Calvert chose finally to declare his Catholic faith. He was not forced to resign because of his conversion; the two actions were not as directly connected as has generally been portrayed.

Not at all a victim of religious persecution; as a mark of continued royal favor and to counter any possible tinge of disgrace, Calvert was named Baron Baltimore. The name derived from a shrine that defined a village in southwestern Ireland (Baal-t-mor devoted to the god Baal). He also retained his position as a member on the Privy Council. With removal of a religious requirement by favor of the king, he retained extensive land grants and other investments such as the Virginia Company and the East India Company.

However, with the accession of Charles I in 1625, Lord Baltimore's status changed. Now having declared himself an open Catholic, he had to resign his position on the Privy Council when a more stringent anti-Catholic policy became effective. He entered into a new career as a capitalist and colonial Catholic entrepreneur, eventually to found a colony on the Chesapeake after a settlement in Newfoundland called "Avalon" failed to succeed.

Despite his open Catholicism, he received land north of the earlier settlement of Virginia. The politic choice of the colony's name of Maryland was in honor of the Queen Henrietta Maria, the French Catholic consort of Charles I. With the death of his father, Cecil Calvert, the namesake of his father's patron, became the 2nd Lord Baltimore. Also, a student at Trinity College at Oxford, he was not able to graduate since such would require an oath of adherence to the Protestant faith. He married Anne Arundel, the daughter of the Catholic Lord Arundel, his father's close friend, after whom the county in Maryland was named.

The younger brother Leonard Calvert was sent to found their colony. The goal was not only to provide a sanctuary that could include English Catholics as well as Protestants in the New World but also to advance English national interests against the Dutch encroaching from the Hudson River Valley on the north. The Calvert charter perforce had to provide for freedom for Protestants as well as Catholics, the so-called "Maryland Design." Unique for its time, there was to be no governmental support of either of the Christian religions (with intolerance for Jews to be remedied only in the 1820s). The extensive potentially lucrative land grant was a testimony to the Calvert family skill in reconciling their Catholicism with their Englishness.

Leonard Calvert founded the first settlement at Saint Mary's City in 1642. As his personal fief without direct control by London until 1691, the Lord Proprietor was free to do as he wished, including the imposition of a manorial system that assigned grants of land as large as a thousand acres to those bringing men to work the land. Given the nature of the provincial English Catholic gentry, their younger sons would provide the largest number of potential Catholic immigrants. However, in marked contrast to the Anglican Virginia and Puritan Massachusetts, religion remained a private endeavor that concerned the government only when it became disruptive. This was the "Maryland Design" to maintain religious peace.

The battle in England between the king and the Puritan Parliament in the 1640s jeopardized the royalist Calvert position as Proprietors in Maryland. Their highly politic "Act of Toleration" in 1649 formalized allegiance to the Proprietor based only "upon the oath of a Christian." Despite this precaution, the temporary removal of the Baltimore proprietorship in the 1650s coincided with the advent of Cromwell in England. Reinstated under the Stuart Restoration in 1660, the relaxation of Catholic persecution under the Stuarts was evidenced by the rebuilding of St Mary's City with its ornate chapel and Capitol.

The increased Protestant population of Maryland particularly in Anne Arundel County coupled with the deposition of the Catholic James II in 1689 brought about the deposition of the 3rd Lord Baltimore around that same time. After the suspension of proprietary rule and royal control, the legislature established the Church of

England with a tax imposed to support it. Despite much opposition from Quakers and Roman Catholics, a tithe was finally signed into law in 1701. There was later a reinstatement of the Calvert family Proprietorship following the conversion of the Calvert family to Protestantism in 1715 that lasted until the American Revolution. Although the early experiment of religious toleration extended by the Lords Baltimore had ended, it eventually found expression in the principles of the U.S. Constitution that further uncoupled religion from politics.

Street names such as Wolfe and Montcalm recognized the opposing generals at Quebec in 1759 during the French and Indian War. Other British names remain such as Eden Street for the last royal governor and Harford Road reflecting the illegitimate son of the last Calvert to serve as Proprietor.

The additional street names of a Revolutionary War hero such as Joseph Warren or Marquis de La Fayette and victories at the Battles of Saratoga and Lexington reflect the more recent Revolutionary times. Charles Pratt, Lord Camden, was considered an important supporter of the colonists when, as Lord Chancellor of England he declared invalid the general search warrants. He was recognized by the names of several of the important streets such as Charles, Pratt as well as Camden. Chase was the name of one of the first Supreme Court Justices; Casimir Pulaski was the name of a Polish volunteer to the Continental Army killed at Savannah. The substantial Polish population of East Baltimore in the 20th century provided him with even greater recognition by a monument in Patterson Park, the center of their community.

The Revolutionary War brought prosperity to Baltimore by landing cargoes in the West Indies despite the Spanish blockade and extensive privateering. The war also freed the merchants from the massive debt owed to the British merchants. It also aided development by enabling the break-up of the large estates by eliminating the practice of entail by which properties would be kept intact through the generations. Exemplary was John Eager Howard's 1782 "Addition" on the west side of town extending west to Eutaw Street with Howard Street the north-south axis. The entire area of the addition extended from Warren Street in the south to Saratoga Street in the north. The names given to the streets reflected the family of the landowner and his victory in the Revolutionary War at Eutaw Springs South Carolina under General Nathanael Greene in 1781. The latter's name was also attached to a street in this area. 1786 was a major milestone in the history of the Baltimore street system when the former horseshoe curve of Jones Falls was straightened by a canal that now ran at a forty-five degree angle to the west of Old Town.

The American Revolution not only brought prosperity but a lightening of political restrictions long borne by Catholics with which the Carroll family was highly identified.

1.3. The Carroll Family and the American Revolution

Born in 1661, Charles Carroll "the Settler" left his native Ireland in 1688 to settle first in St Mary's City in Maryland. He was descended from the O'Carrolls, a long line of Irish chieftains whose lands were largely confiscated by Cromwell in the mid-17th century. He was nonetheless well-educated by Jesuits on the European continent under the auspices of his wealthy kinsman Sir Richard Grace.

The appointment of this first Carroll in Maryland to the office of Attorney General of Maryland under the 3rd Lord Baltimore was short-lived. With the accession of the Protestant monarchs William and Mary in 1689, the openly Catholic Calvert Proprietorship was deposed. Despite the loss of political control, the Lords Baltimore remained the largest landowners. Carroll particularly prospered in the service of the Calvert cousin managing the Proprietor's family properties in Maryland. Sir Henry Darnall was also conveniently Carroll's father-in-law.

Although Catholics were denied the right to vote or hold office, by virtue of a series of marriages and the Calvert family sponsorship, Charles Carroll "the Settler" amassed both great liquid wealth and landholdings. The latter amounted to nearly 60,000 acres mainly in Anne Arundel/Baltimore and Prince George's Counties by the time of his death in 1720. He accomplished this feat while retaining both his religion and his devotion to the Jacobite Stuart cause.

The two living sons, Charles and Daniel Carroll, were enjoined to nurture the estate and their commitment to the causes of their Irish forbearers. Indeed, they were instructed by their father to sign themselves as "Marylando-Hibernus" on their writings at the Jesuit College of St Omer in Flanders. They were the progenitors of the two Carroll lines so prominent in the history of the area well into the 19th century.

The elder styled as "of Annapolis," showed less pretension and less profligacy than his brother Daniel and the latter's heirs. In light of the depression in tobacco prices in the 1720s, the brothers invested in the iron making Baltimore Company in association with their Protestant "Barrister" cousins that used the property eventually called "Mount Clare." The lower watershed of Gwynns Falls was denuded to provide the fuel for the furnaces before they closed in 1810.

The Charles Carroll of this generation carried out an active collection of rents and loans at compound interest to the benefit of his own personal financial interests even in managing his brother's estate for the benefit of his nephews in their minority. These activities led to an acrimonious dispute with his nephew Daniel Carroll "of Duddington Manor" re the stewardship of the nephew's interests. The latter's estate in Prince George's County became a prominent one in what was to be the Capitol Hill area of the District of Columbia.

As yet, without an heir of his own, Charles Carroll of Annapolis developed a relationship with Elizabeth Brooke that produced a potential heir in 1737. However, their marriage did not take place until 1757. This irregular arrangement served Carroll's single minded fulfillment of the responsibilities enjoined upon him. The upbringing of their son Charles Carroll, later styled "of Carrollton," became a major focus of the life of the father to insure the appropriateness of his son inheriting the Carroll fortune. The standing of the son as an heir remained tentative and would not actually occur until 1757 when his parents' marriage legitimized his birth; and when his education and behavior had apparently met his father's expectations.

CHARLES CARROLL OF CARROLLTON.

Fig. 3 – Charles Carroll of Carrollton

The younger Carroll's education was also carried out under Jesuit auspices at St Omer in Flanders, favored by Maryland Catholic gentry, but also at the College of the Jesuits at Rheims and then Bourges. This was followed by attendance at the College of St Louis-le-Grand in Paris; and then the study of law in London before returning to Maryland to receive recognition as heir. The long-time anomalous common-law marriage arrangement also deprived Elizabeth Brooke of potential dower rights that might have led, on the not unexpected occasion of widowhood and remarriage, to the alienation of a significant portion of the Carroll property to a subsequent marriage partner, possibly even a Protestant.

Politically disenfranchised, the Carroll wealth made them all the more vulnerable to discrimination, particularly when England was at war with Catholic foreign powers such as France or Spain and their loyalty was questioned. For example, during the Seven Years War with France (1756-1763), Carroll strongly considered transferring his assets to Louisiana, then still under Catholic French control. On his return to Maryland from his education abroad, young Charles Carroll discouraged his father from doing so. He considered the religious persecution to which they were subjected less severe than the loss of liberty that might ensue under a Catholic monarch. Having received the estate of Carrollton on the Monocacy River in Frederick County, he was subsequently styled as "of Carrollton."

The ongoing battles over the imposition of taxes by the British Parliament starting with the Stamp Act in 1765 offered an opportunity for young Carroll to enter directly into political life for the first time. The political situation in Maryland differed from that of any other colony. Far greater even than the Penn's in Pennsylvania, the feudal power of the Calvert's and their patronage controlled political life. The "court party," made up of appointees beholden to the Proprietor controlled the upper council of the legislature; the gentry (country party) represented in the lower house (Assembly) increasingly sought power rather than patronage.

The Assembly supported Maryland's representation at the Stamp Act Congress called by Samuel Adams of Massachusetts. Later, affected primarily by opposition to the continued role of the Proprietor, there was increased support by Maryland for the other colonies in respect to the Townsend Acts and in opposition to the closing of the Port of Boston in 1774. In the fall of 1774, the *Peggy Stewart* brought tea into Annapolis that was burned along with the ship. It could be said that "Annapolis out-Bostoned Boston."

Charles Carroll of Carrollton elected to join the country party, albeit its most conservative wing. Merely an observer to the 1st Continental Congress in 1774, Carroll became a member of the Maryland Committee of Correspondence and, finally an official delegate to the 2nd Continental Congress in 1776 that issued the Declaration of Independence. A Catholic, he had nonetheless been elected for the first time to public office obviating the prohibition on voting and office holding that had long been in effect. The old discriminatory laws against Catholics were now no longer in effect.

Elected to the 1st U.S. Senate, he served along with his cousins Daniel Carroll in the House of Representatives and Bishop John Carroll. All had important roles in securing the passage of the 1st Amendment that guaranteed religious liberty for the new republic, consistent with the principle of Maryland from its founding but long held in abeyance.

The deaths of John Adams and Thomas Jefferson in 1826 on the 50th anniversary of the Declaration of Independence left Carroll standing as one of the few remaining Founders. At the end of his long life in 1832, Charles Carroll "of Carrollton" had became famous as the only Catholic signer and ultimately had the distinction as "the last living Signer of the Declaration of Independence," a figure in the legend of the Revolution.

Fig. 4 - Homewood

Charles Carroll's son, Charles Carroll Jr used his family fortune to leave his mark by building the still extant mansion called "Homewood," in the early Federal style patterned after Robert Adam. Contrary to his father's wishes, the cost of the house mounted to an extent that their relations were severely strained. It became the property of the Wyman family, hence the name Wyman Park for that area surrounding Homewood. The first home of the Gilman School for Boys; now part of the Johns Hopkins University campus, the design of the Homewood house provides the pattern for the other subsequent university buildings.

The American Revolution thus freed Carroll to become a leader of the new republic. Although missing the actual vote on the Declaration, Carroll is credited in changing the instructions to the

Maryland delegation from that of opposition to the support for independence. He was also available for the signing of the Declaration. Religious and ethnic tolerance achieved during the American Revolution seemed to open the electorate for the first time to Catholics and Germans. It is estimated that Catholics comprised about 2% of the population. Germans had been excluded as alien-born, regardless of naturalization, from holding office although not from voting.

Charles Carroll, in accordance with his class interests, led in restricting the franchise to the relatively small number of the propertied with the passage of a conservative Maryland state constitution in 1776. The Maryland state government remained in the hands of the propertied class with a high property requirement for voting and holding office. Universal male suffrage was achieved in 1801; property qualifications for office holding were removed in 1810. Delegates from Baltimore City were admitted for the first time with the constitution and several new counties were created. However, representation was not based on population so that the more populous areas did not receive appropriate representation; slaves were not taxed at the same high rate as other property, yet slaves were fully counted for representation in the Maryland Assembly. This was a recurrent problem for Baltimore that gave disproportionate representation in the Maryland Assembly to the agricultural interests of southern Maryland and the Eastern Shore with large slave-holdings.

It is important to recognize that Baltimore was in but not of a slave holding society. The large rural slaveholders consistently denied Baltimore adequate representation in state politics. Their interests in maintaining the discipline of racially-based agricultural slavery differed from the wage-labor occupational character of both the free and slave blacks in the city.

The expansion of the town was reflected by the Broadway Market at Fells Point on the east supplemented in the 1780s by the Center (Marsh) Market on the site of Harrison's Marsh between Baltimore Town and Jones's Town with the Lexington Market on the west. The Camden Market served the farthest western part of town including Federal Hill. The truck farms of East Baltimore was the major source of the food brought in daily to the public markets.

Prominent at Charles and Saratoga Streets during this time was the site of the first brick building of Old St Paul's Anglican Church from which St Paul's Street eventually received its name. The Methodists under Francis Asbury at the Christmas Conference of 1784 voted to separate from the Anglican Church to found the Methodist Episcopal Church in America at the Lovely Lane Church. With the Methodists and Quakers supportive of slave rights but nevertheless discriminatory in practice, by 1797 the relatively large free black community founded Bethel A.M.E. the first of the African Methodist Episcopal Churches and in 1802 the Sharp Street Methodist Episcopal Church.

The great Greek revival domed cube building of the First Unitarian Church on Franklin and Charles Street was designed by

Maximilian Godefroy. At its dedication in 1819, the Boston-based William Ellery Channing preached his famous "Baltimore Sermon" that defined the tenets of Unitarianism to the close-knit transplanted New Englanders. Godefroy, born in France in 1765, trained as a civil engineer. A Royalist during the French Revolution and then an anti-Bonapartist, he was imprisoned until 1805. He arrived in Baltimore the following year where he was an instructor in art and architecture at St Mary's College, run by the Sulpician Order, also in flight from the French Revolution. That same order also ran St Mary's Seminary, the first in the United States founded in 1795 and, in the French Gallican model, contributed to the relative independence from Rome of the American Catholic Church. Associated with the fellow architect Benjamin Henry Latrobe for a time, Godefroy independently designed the chapel of St Mary's, the Unitarian Church and the Battle Monument during his stay in Baltimore before his return to France after the Bourbon Restoration in 1819.

1.4. Archbishop John Carroll and the Catholic Church

By 1806, the Basilica of the Assumption of the Virgin Mary had been started to become the seat of John Carroll, the first American Catholic archbishop. Gothic was still too radical and unfamiliar for such an important building; Carroll chose a classical design of a basilica in the Greek design. In the form of a Greek cross with the dome designed by Benjamin Henry Latrobe, lit from above, the architect reproduced the Pantheon within the Parthenon.

The Baltimore Cathedral was completed after the archbishop's death in 1815. Its prominent site denoted the importance of Maryland's Catholic heritage. Now called the Basilica of the Assumption, the seat of the archbishop has moved to Upper Charles Street on the edge of the Guilford-Homeland-Roland Park District. The Cathedral of Mary Our Queen was built as a result of a bequest by Thomas O'Neill, a native of County Cavan Ireland who immigrated to Baltimore in 1866. One of eight children, his fortune came from O'Neill's Department Store at Charles and Lexington Streets, miraculously saved from destruction at the time of the Great Baltimore Fire of 1904.

Fig. 5 - Basilica of the Assumption

John Carroll was born in 1735 on his maternal family's estate of "Darnall's Chance" in Upper Marlborough in Prince George's County. He was the second son of Daniel Carroll, the younger of the two sons of Charles Carroll "the Settler." John Carroll's elder brother Daniel Carroll "of Duddington" has already entered our story as the nephew and ward during his minority of Charles Carroll of Annapolis. Both brothers were thus first cousins to Charles Carroll of Carrollton but somewhat less endowed with riches. For example, in 1790 the heirs of Daniel Carroll owned 53 slaves rather than the 316 owned by the senior branch.

Fig. 6 - Archbishop John Carroll

Like his cousin Charles Carroll of Carrollton, John Carroll was educated at the Jesuit College at St Omer in Belgium established to educate the sons of English Catholic gentry. Joining the Jesuits in

1753 at age eighteen, he trained at the University of Liege before his ordination in 1769. Father Carroll returned to the United States in 1773 after the suppression of his order by the Pope. It is estimated that the total Catholic population at that time was 36,000, mainly in Maryland and less than 2% of the white population of the entire country.

In Maryland, Carroll acted as a missionary priest establishing the first Catholic parish of St John the Evangelist in what is now Forest Glen Maryland. During the Revolution, American Catholics remained under the jurisdiction of the Bishop of London who foreswore any connection with the rebels. It was thus possible to consider the development of the American church directly with Rome, free of British taint. Moreover, in the context of the religious freedom created by the American Revolution, Father Carroll was able to found at Whitemarsh Plantation at Bowie Maryland in 1783 the Catholic Church in the United States. In a move unique to the United States, Father Carroll was elected by his fellow priests and only then in 1784, confirmed by Pope Pius VI to be the Prefect Apostolic, Superior of the Missions in the United States.

In 1789, after the formation of the United States and following the model of the newly formed "Episcopal Church of the United States" as well as what was called the "American Methodist Church," Carroll felt free to become the first Catholic bishop of the Catholic Church. He was ordained as bishop on August 15th 1790 (The Feast of the Assumption) and took his seat in Baltimore at the Church of St Peter. In 1792, the second Catholic parish of St Patrick's was established at Fell's Point in Baltimore. In 1808, Carroll was ordained by Pius VII as the first American archbishop of the Archdiocese of Baltimore, then encompassing the entire area of the original thirteen colonies. Suffragan bishops were invested by him in Boston, New York, Philadelphia and Bardstown Kentucky.

Baltimore was a commercial city whose naval heritage was at its height during this era. The U. S. Congress authorized in 1794 the building of six frigates that were the foundation of the U.S. Navy. Following the design of Philadelphia shipwright Joshua Humphreys, the heavier than usual American frigates were a hybrid between the larger "ship-of-the-line" and an ordinary frigate. Throughout the 1790s, this building program moved forward in response to the threats offered by the Algerian Barbary Pirates; then after peace was declared in 1796, with the threat by the French in the "Quasi-War" in 1798. Each of the ships was built in a different port in private shipyards. Closely identified with Baltimore was the 36-gun frigate *USS Constellation* built at Stodder's shipyard in Fell's Point in 1797. As a reminder, the much rebuilt sailing ship of that name remains tied up in the Inner Harbor.

Fig. 7 - The *U.S.S. Constellation*

The famed Baltimore clipper fleet built at Fells Point carried on a coastal trade with an easy conversion to privateers during the War of 1812. These "sharp built" schooners built in Baltimore for the West Indian trade had light hulls that could cut through the water and were heavily fitted with canvass. The ships had great speed from the ability to sail close to the wind; hence, the name of "clipper." They were ideal for use in the less stormy South Atlantic and the Caribbean where they were used. Sail duck was another Baltimore specialty of its mills along the watercourses that complemented the shipbuilding industry at Fells Point.

Based on the commerce carried in these swift ships, the city tripled in size between 1785 and 1815. The continental wars starting in 1793 following the French Revolution increased the need for foodstuffs in Europe. After 1800, the war in Spain also increased the need of the British Army for grain. For example, in 1811 Baltimore ships unloaded almost 400,000 barrels of flour at Cadiz or Lisbon that collected a 100% profit over the price at home. Overall, American exports, of which Baltimore reaped a significant proportion of the total, rose from $20 million in 1790 to $70 million in 1800. By 1810, Baltimore's population approached 50,000; many of those emigrating from the counties of eastern and southern Maryland adjoining the Chesapeake Bay included skilled mariners and ship builders.

The "peaceful coercive acts" of the Jefferson and Madison Administrations limiting imports from Britain were generally supported in Baltimore; its major trade was with the West Indies. There was also wide support for the declaration of war in June 1812 that could lead to profitable privateering by Baltimore's fast ships. The majority of the city was allied to the Democratic-Republicans. The Federalist *Federal Republican* newspaper was opposed to the war. The newspaper office was trashed by a riotous mob that then retired. Eventually, as Federalists became armed in an effort to reassert their right to freedom of the press, the jail where men had been taken for safekeeping was also attacked by the mob. One man was killed and the Revolutionary War General Lighthorse Harry Lee (father of Robert E. Lee) was severely injured, never to recover fully.

This new level of rioting in 1812 departed from the short term and more limited character of earlier times such as carried out by the Sons of Liberty. No longer could the crowd be brought under control by merely "reading the riot act" by community leaders.

Rather violence now lasted for several weeks and included far more far ranging attacks beyond the initial attack on the newspaper. There were attacks on free blacks and between Catholics and Protestants that reflected the more diverse city that no longer had a sense of comity. It was the first of a series of riots that earned Baltimore the title of "Mobtown" and became a major social problem. The use of military force and the development of urban police were the results of this breakdown of social order that appeared in Baltimore to such an unusual degree, presaging its later history.

Immediately after the declaration of war in June 1812, ships were converted and armed. There were approximately two hundred persons who acted as the major investors; fifty of whom were the most active with the firms of John Hollins and that of Samuel Smith the most prominent. These same persons had also been prominent in trading prior to the War. Among the mercantile elite were names that still remain known on the map of Baltimore such as Hollins, McCulloch, Patterson and Sheppard with several benefiting from gains as high as nearly $500,000. One of the leading traders as well as political and military leaders was Samuel Smith.

1.5. Samuel Smith and the War of 1812

Fig. 8 - Samuel Smith

Maryland's Senator Samuel Smith was born in Carlisle Pennsylvania in 1752. His grandfather of the same name had first come to Lancaster County from Northern Ireland in 1729. His father John Smith moved to Baltimore in the 1760s as part of the first migration of Scotch-Irish Presbyterians from Pennsylvania and later from Ulster that further defined the character of the city. The tall spire of the First Presbyterian Church at Madison Street and Park Avenue still commands the western boundary of the fashionable Mt Vernon area vying with the equally tall spire of the Mt Vernon United

Methodist Church dominating Monument Square, the two largest Protestant denominations.

The firm of Smith and Buchanan became prosperous with a thousand foot wharf extending into the harbor, the city's only until 1782. Samuel Smith entered the family firm when aged fourteen after a sketchy education. Despite his youth, he was able to travel independently in Europe on business for the family firm.

An officer in the Continental Army until 1778, he rose to the rank of Lieutenant Colonel of the crack 1st Regiment of the Maryland "Old Line" during the campaigns of 1776 and 1777. He was particularly noted for his stalwart defense of Fort Mifflin in the fall of 1777on the Delaware River blocking the British force occupying Philadelphia. He spent the bitter winter of 1777-1778 at Valley Forge before leading his troops at the Battle of Monmouth.

Back in Baltimore, he was appointed Brigadier-General in the Maryland militia while reconstituting his fortune via privateering as well as by profits from provisioning the force reaching Yorktown in 1781 to besiege Cornwallis. Now one of the town's most prominent citizens, Smith commanded the Maryland militia quota in the 1794 Whisky Rebellion under the overall command of Lighthorse Harry Lee.

A member of Congress starting in 1793 initially as a Federalist, he opposed the Jay Treaty of 1795 as detrimental to Baltimore's extensive trade to the West Indies. He helped the presidential candidacy of Jefferson in 1800 and became senator in 1803 as a

Republican-Democrat. Despite his being one of the wealthiest men in Baltimore, he was the popular candidate of the mass of mechanics, sailors and dockworkers. As the commander of the militia, he also had their support. In turn, he advocated lowering the property requirements for voting and office holding and made Baltimore a Republican bastion in an otherwise Federalist Maryland.

Baltimore under Smith's leadership had supported the embargo instituted by Jefferson. He had believed, based on his own commercial experience that their interests in the sugar islands would force the European powers to capitulate to American demands. The leader of a loosely defined group of dissident Republicans in the Congress called "The Invisibles," he was consistent in supporting naval defense expenditures. He opposed the appointment of Secretary of the Treasury Gallatin as secretary of state under President Madison. The conflict came to a head when Smith successfully opposed the re-charter of the Bank of the United States that had been sponsored by Gallatin. His brother Robert Smith was forced to resign his cabinet position as secretary of state in favor of James Monroe and the power of his faction was reduced.

In the 12th "War Congress" meeting in December 1811, the "Invisibles" under a Smith ally opposed the "shilly-shallying" of Madison and, in alliance with Henry Clay, favored preparation for war, accomplished in June 1812. As major-general of the Maryland militia, from early 1813 General Smith also led in the preparation of the defenses of Baltimore, clearly a British objective because of the impact on their shipping by the privateers based there.

The political career of Samuel Smith was temporarily eclipsed when the Federalist majority in the state assembly in 1814 failed to re-elect him to the U.S. Senate. He was however returned to the U.S. House of Representatives and later to the Senate. A long-time supporter of the Jacksonian Democrats, he was acclaimed as the city's first citizen. Smith died in his eighty-eighth year with his funeral procession appropriately led by President Martin Van Buren and his cabinet, Andrew Jackson's protégé and successor.

During 1813, British Vice-Admiral George Cockburn had been raiding up and down the blockaded Chesapeake Bay. He had gained a hard-bitten reputation for destroying coastal settlements around the bay. On April 16th, the British approached the entrance to the Patapsco Northwest Branch. General Smith had strengthened Fort McHenry fortified by 42 pounder cannon taken off an abandoned French-man-of-war. Among the men working the batteries were free blacks welcomed in the navy if not in the militia. With the American ships in the harbor protected by the fort, the British withdrew to attack further north and destroy Havre de Grace in Harford County. Once again, there was an approach to Baltimore in August 1813 before withdrawing to attack St Michaels in Talbot County on the Eastern Shore.

After nearly two years of war, by 1814 the British had clearly embarked on a "hard war" on the American towns subject to naval incursions. The goal was to inflict such pain so as to bring home to the population the cost of waging war. With the defeat of Napoleon at the Battle of Leipzig in the fall of 1813, British land forces were now freed up to participate in more sustained attacks. An attack on the City of Washington, hardly of strategic value, would be compatible with what was essentially a "terrorist campaign." Based on his sense of the unimportance of what only recently had become the national capital, Secretary of War John Armstrong had consistently deprecated the likelihood of any attack. A recurrent attack on the more significant port and commercial city of Baltimore appeared more likely to Armstrong.

However, by the morning of the 24th of August 1814, two groups were indeed marching on Washington. There were 4000 veteran infantry and artillerymen of the British Army commanded by Major General Robert Ross, a veteran of Wellington's Peninsular campaign, and a 500 man detachment of sailors and marines under Rear Admiral George Cockburn. The British Atlantic Fleet under Vice-Admiral Alexander Cochrane had bypassed Fort Washington protecting Washington on the Potomac River. Cochrane moved his fleet up the Patuxent River fifteen to twenty miles to the east and landed troops at Benedict twenty miles upstream on the 18th August.

Marching across land, Cockburn had bottled up Commodore Joshua Barney's little fleet of American gunboats on the Patuxent and forced Barney to scuttle them on 22nd August. By August 21st when the British landing force under Ross had reached Upper Marlboro, it was clear that their objective was not Baltimore but the unprepared and relatively undefended national capital. Upper Marlboro in Prince George's County was just a day's march away from Washington.

The American commanding general, still unclear as to the direction to be taken by the British, had only 2000 untrained militia to oppose the British advance. On 24th August, the British came to Bladensburg, approaching the city from the northeast where the bridge was still intact across the Eastern Branch of the Potomac. Frightened by the British use of rockets, the inexperienced militia ran. The Battle of Bladensburg was quickly over and the road to Washington was open.

After the debacle at Bladensburg, the initial decision was to try to take a stand on the Heights of Georgetown to the west of the city. This left open to the enemy the U.S. Capitol as well as the President's House. With the Capitol alight since 6:30 that night and still burning, by 10:30 on the night of the 24th, the British advance party was at the deserted President's House. Piling up the furniture and the draperies in each room, fires were lit. Next, the Treasury Building to the east went up in flames; the State and War Department Building to the west was burned the next morning. The British commanders remained concerned that their accompanying flotilla had not come up the Potomac. The British force therefore left during the night of the 25th August after only one day's occupation.

After uniting with their flotilla downstream, the British prepared to attack Baltimore by sea. Unlike Washington City, there had long been an expectation of a British attack. During 1813, General Smith had equipped his militia men with muskets and instituted regular drills of those working the guns at Fort McHenry. By the summer of 1814, he had enlisted as many as 15,000 men including both slaves and their owners in the building of entrenchments on Hampstead Hill and at Patapsco Point.

On 12th September, British Major General Robert Ross landed his army of 4500 at North Point, where Smith had predicted they would land and was thus prepared to oppose them. They were met by defenders at a narrow point on the peninsula leading to the city. In the ensuing Battle of North Point, the British incurred heavy casualties including the death of their commander.

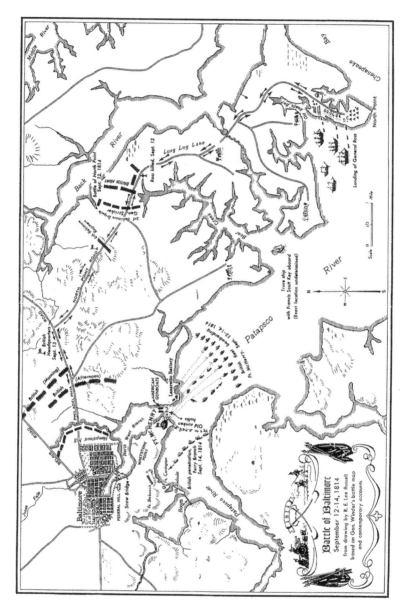

Fig. 9 – Battle of Baltimore

On 13th September, the British army force arrived at the eastern Baltimore town limits to find the Americans under the command of Samuel Smith well-entrenched on Hampstead Hill (now part of Patterson Park.) During the night of September 13th-14th, the British fleet had been unable to bypass Fort McHenry under Major George Armistead guarding the entrance to the harbor. Despite the bombardment throughout the night, the "Stars and Stripes" still remained in the morning light to be witnessed by Francis Scott Key.

Without naval support from their fleet that had been held up by Fort McHenry, the British were unable to land another force to attack the entrenchments at Hampstead Hill from the flank. Another British effort to land a force to the west along the Middle Branch to flank Fort McHenry also failed. They decided to withdraw. This defeat, along with that at Plattsburg on Lake Champlain emboldened the American Peace Commissioners at Ghent to overcome the effects of the capture of Washington. The Treaty of Ghent ended the war under more favorable terms than previously expected.

The Baltimore County Courthouse moved from Joppa in 1768 to be situated atop a cliff at Calvert Street in Baltimore City. (Old Court Road remains to recognize that connection to the courthouse at Joppa.) By 1784, the town had grown northward so that Calvert Street had to be extended beneath the courthouse that was now raised to accommodate the extension of the street. The building of the succeeding Baltimore City Courthouse and then City Hall still remains on that site between Fayette and Lexington Streets surrounding since 1815 Maximilian Godefroy's Battle Monument.

Commemorating the Battle of Baltimore in 1814, it remains the motto of the city of Baltimore.

Fig. 10 - The Battle Monument

The base is an Egyptian Revival cenotaph surmounted by a column shaped like a Roman fasces innovative in that it is inscribed with the names of those who died at Fort McHenry and North Point rather than some surviving general or politician. At the top is a female figure with a laurel wreath that has since symbolized the city of Baltimore.

Two other more conventional monuments were commissioned in 1914 at the time of the centennial of the battle. A standing portrait statue of General Samuel Smith by Hans Schuler, a prolific local sculptor, marks what at the time of the Battle of Baltimore had been a gun battery on Federal Hill. Within the same park stands a statue of Lt Colonel George Armistead, the commander of Fort McHenry during the bombardment. He is particularly recognized for commissioning the unusually large U.S. ensign that became immortalized as the "Start Spangled Banner." The sculptor Edward Berge was also a local sculptor. Both these local sculptors trained together originally in Baltimore and then in Paris before returning to Baltimore for the major part of their career at the Maryland Institute of Art.

As development spread from the original town laid out on the harbor basin, the layers of the city's growth can be read like a series of concentric rings around the central core. Like Philadelphia, and even before that like London, the housing pattern of row houses in Baltimore became predominant using locally made bricks from the clay soil and locally cut marble for the front steps. Nowhere else in the United States has the row house been employed with such persistence. At each stage in this development, the row house varied in its architectural design and its degree of ornamentation. Usually built for the working class by builders, yet their design responded to the style of the more ornate row houses and even detached houses being designed simultaneously by architects for those who were the rich. The style of the working class row house evolved from federal to Greek revival from 1820 through the 1850s to the Italianate after the 1860s.

Normally built to the street line, the uniform blocks of houses varied in their width, depth and height depending on the lot size, whether facing on to the front or to the alley on the rear or even grander when facing a park. Built by speculators on land leased usually for 99 years, they could thus be priced low enough, establishing a pattern of white owner-occupied housing. By the 1820s, Baltimore had become the third largest town in the United States, outstripping even Boston and Charleston and, thanks to immigration, remained in the front rank along with New York and Philadelphia for much of the 19th century.

Fig. 11 - Baltimore Row Houses

The end of the narrow peninsula dividing the Middle Branch from Northwest Harbor, Whetstone Point (named after the smooth stone found there) was the site of what became in the 1798 a fort named after then Secretary of War and leading Maryland Federalist James McHenry. Federal Hill, named after the 1789 ratification of the U.S. Constitution, is at the northeast corner of that peninsula overlooking the Inner Harbor. It was developed with housing from the edge of the harbor southward.

Its working class row houses can illustrate that of other parts of the city. The land to the north owned by John Eager Howard was mainly laid out in lots and built upon by 1820 in the federal style characterized by gable roofs and dormer windows. To the south, land owned by the Moale family was next to being developed. Starting in the 1840s, smaller houses were built for rental to accommodate the mainly German newly arrived immigrants or to be sold to small tradesmen. Only a thin one-brick party wall separated the houses, lath and plaster wall separating the attics and there was a continuous roof. Interiors began to reflect Greek revival motifs with woodwork containing concentric circles emulating the more complex decoration of the higher-priced housing being built to the north on the city's hills.

In a similar fashion, emulating the style used elsewhere for higher priced brownstone housing, after the Civil War land further to the south was covered with two-story narrow-front Italianate style housing characterized by tall narrow first floor windows, window lintels and roof cornices with flat or slightly sloping roofs. This style extended into South Baltimore beyond the confines of Federal Hill area. Like other areas throughout Baltimore, their low cost enabled working class buyers to take possession buttressed by the building associations developed within their ethnic communities. Baltimore began to develop its unique character.

CHAPTER 2
BALTIMORE CITY 1815-1865

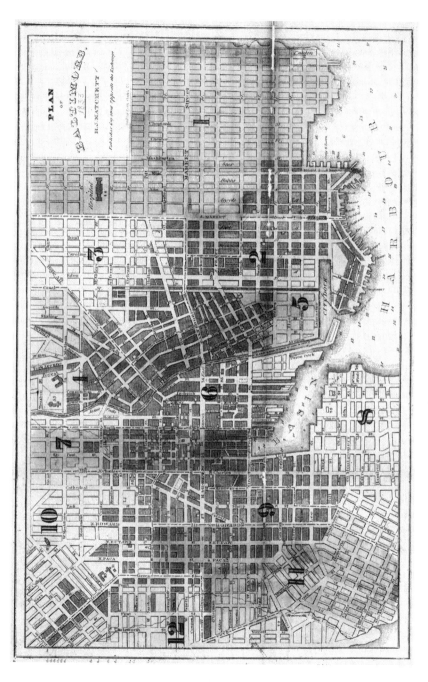

Fig. 12 - Baltimore 1833

The adjoining map shows the development of the city following the Poppleton Plan of the 1820s. Although the boundary reached to what is North Avenue, the streets reach north only to the borders of Monument Square. The four boulevard squares laid out by the Howard heirs included the north-south Washington Place and the house lots on the east-west Mount Vernon Place; the latter gave its name to the entire area.

1.1. The Mercantile City /To North Avenue (Boundary Road)

The population nearly doubled from 1810 in a decade reaching 62,000 by 1820, to 102,000 in 1840 and 212,999 by 1860; the second largest city in the nation, it edged out Philadelphia. Baltimore was similar to New York in having a large amount of land to fill in without need for annexation. The boundaries of the city had expanded to incorporate eighteen square miles of the county in 1816 to be platted by Thomas Poppleton in accordance with the need to support real estate development. However, by 1837, development had occurred along Calvert Street only to Madison Street; the southwest limit was at Paca and Lexington Streets; the northwest limit was Poppleton and Franklin Streets; Federal Hill was limited to the area bordering the waterfront. Paca Street was named after William Paca, born in Harford County in 1740 of the local planter elite. He graduated from the forerunner of the University of Pennsylvania in 1759, practiced law in Annapolis and became a member of the Continental Congress from 1774 to 1779 when he was a signer of the Declaration of Independence. Later he became Justice of the Maryland Court and Governor in 1782.

The British blockade of the Chesapeake during the War of 1812 had severely limited trade while encouraging the early development of local industry. The generation after the end of the War of 1812 was marked by prosperity with the development of the far more efficient steam driven industry in addition to the existing water driven mills. Textile mills joined the former flour mills and iron forges that could be situated anywhere, no longer limited to the watercourses.

William J. Dickey came to Baltimore in the 1830s from Ballymena in Northern Ireland. He first operated on a shoestring by "putting out" wool to be woven by housewives; then in 1870s took over the former Wethered Woolen Mill on Gwynns Fall; the town surrounding them was later renamed in his honor Dickeyville as it still remains, now restored. Originally, a paper mill in the 18th century, the Wethered family converted it to textiles in the 1830s as the Ashland Mills. Still another major industry was at "Avalon," an ironworks famous for its nails organized by the Ellicott brothers to complement their other mills on the Patapsco. Other mills processed imported coffee, sugar and copper adjacent to the port.

Despite the prosperity of the middle class, the plight of the white working class whether native or immigrant, male or female, was not at all easy, let alone that of the black free or enslaved. Whether white or black, unskilled labor functioned at low subsistence wages that insured control by the owners of capital the freedom to dispose of them. The ethos of the time was that there was a self-regulating economy that stressed the opportunities available to the industrious and the temperate.

The jobs available included the publicly funded need to keep the shallow Inner Harbor free of the silt and muck that continually filled it. For example, from 1790 onward, the city funded a "mud machine" to cut a channel through the mud bar that formed. Often forced to stand in the shallow water, fifty or sixty men waited for the melting of the ice to work nine months a year guiding the scoop that emptied the muck into the waiting scows at the pay rate of $1. per day.

The transition from the mercantile to the industrial city was incomplete. In the 1830s, most industrial establishments were still small, run by artisans but also employing unskilled labor and the young apprentices performing the harder labor near the old commercial center. There were the beginnings of the enlargement of the existing workshops such as breweries, forges and shipyards using unskilled labor with some separation of the residence from the workshop for the more affluent. By the end of this era in 1860, specific industrial areas have already begun to arise at the periphery of the old commercial district near the wharves. Baltimore's first large industrial estate along the waterfront east of Fells Point was named after the source of the O'Donnell trading fortune made in a 1785 voyage to Canton China. With the rise of steam driven factories and the need to walk to work, there were also the beginnings of the formation of the more fragmented cellular city that Baltimore was to become in the next generation.

The National Road, the first of the major governmental internal improvements, led from Baltimore west via the Frederick Turnpike through the Cumberland Gap to Wheeling on the Ohio River.

Continuous trains of Conestoga wagons brought lumber, flour and pork east and groceries and dry goods west. The central carriageway was composed of stone and gravel on a cleared right of way four rods wide. By 1833, the road had reached Columbus Ohio on its way to Vandalia, the then capital city of Illinois. Coastal steamers also connected Baltimore to its other major market to the South.

From the original sixty acres in 1729, the town boundaries had grown to nearly 800 aces by 1780 and 13.2 square miles in its first major annexation in 1816. Until then, there had been no overall plan for the city's previously haphazard physical expansion. The only major east-west street was the highly congested "Market Street" (later Baltimore Street). Land had been laid out in response to the wishes of the owners under a loose system controlled by the state legislature in Annapolis with only occasional concern for adjoining roads to be connected.

In 1784, the Town Commissioners were first authorized to make a survey of the city and to regulate the streets had been "heretofore laid out so negligently as to not conform to the other streets." This was not completed until 1795, prior to the incorporation of the city in 1797. Maps were created to be sold by private subscription but were not definitive. Long postponed, the commission to create an accurate property map was given to Thomas Poppleton to be accepted only in 1823 to deal with the newly annexed portion but not the older portions of the town. That plat plan remained until the next major annexation in 1888. Around the same time, for the first time, a hydrographic survey was authorized of the harbor showing channels and depths as affected by the multiple wharves already built and the silting that had occurred.

Further annexation to Baltimore City from Baltimore County began to be considered in the mid-19th century as farmland was increasingly converted to housing. A developed belt of land wrapped around the boundaries of the city that had been established in 1817. There was clear need for municipal type services but concomitant increase in taxes to pay for such services was a long delayed unacceptable trade-off. The belt population approached 40,000 before annexation occurred one mile farther in the north and west in 1888 but not in the east and south until 1918. There has been no subsequent annexation.

Unlike cities such as Washington DC that were planned at the outset, the story of Baltimore, like most other older American cities, was a mix of an uneven planning. The grid was superimposed regardless of topographical features while leaving intact the previous older unplanned section. Successive streets were named after the wealthy landowners or speculative builders who filled the lots with houses. The large number of hills remains perpetuated in names such as Mount Royal (the site of the B&O station on Bolton Hill), Mount Clare (the site of the original B&O station), Mount Washington and Mount Vernon. The stream valleys on both east and west made it more difficult to conform to the use of the grid street pattern modeled as it is are after that of Philadelphia.

John Eager Howard, one of the commissioners overseeing this effort, was one of the largest landowners who left his imprint on

Baltimore. Born in 1752 in Baltimore County to a member of the planter elite, he fought in the Continental Army. Rising to the rank of colonel of the 3rd Maryland Regiment of the "Old Line," he fought with Washington at White Plains, at Monmouth; then with General Nathanael Greene at Guilford Courthouse and Eutaw. He is noted for his leadership in a bayonet charge against the British line at the Battle of Cowpens in South Carolina in 1781. Governor of Maryland from 1789 to 1791, he was Federalist U.S. Senator from 1797 to 1803. Still living at the time of the War of 1812, he opposed any effort to ransom Baltimore rather than fight the British advance against the city in 1814.

An equestrian statue of John Eager Howard as a Revolutionary War general stands in the North Garden of Washington Place. Designed by Emmanuel Fremiet, he was renowned for his equestrian statues including those of Jeanne d'Arc. He was also the successor to Antoine Barye as Artist to the Museum of Natural History in Paris.

Fig. 13 - John Eager Howard Monument

Mount Vernon and Washington Place were carved as building plots out of the Howard estate of Belvedere. The name of the original estate continues in the still extant Beaux-Arts Belvedere Hotel, once the site of the fashionable debutante parties and the Assembly, now a condominium. Charles Howard, the youngest son of Colonel Howard, built in 1829 his mansion northeast of the Monument. By 1842, William Tiffany built a neo-classical house at 8 West Mount Vernon Square. In the 1850s, the lots adjoining the east-west squares were filled the mansions of the rich. They showed the most extravagant houses in the Greek revival style of the 1840s.

Fashion extended like a "fan" to North Avenue along Cathedral, Charles, St Paul and Calvert Streets; northwest along Madison Street and Eutaw Place, all formerly part of the Howard estate. This hilly area benefited from the prevailing northwest winds that freed it from the smells of the industries below. The large houses faced the north-south streets with alleys behind.

John Rudolph Niernsee was the architect most associated with the buildings of Mount Vernon Place and adjoining streets with the intricate ironwork produced in the Baltimore foundries used for architectural decoration.

Born in Vienna in 1814, Niernsee was trained in Prague under stone mason and builder Josef Andreas Kranner, a pioneer in the Gothic Revival. He was also trained at the premier German speaking Prague Polytechnik. Immigrating to the United States in 1836, he was first hired by Benjamin Henry Latrobe II for work on designing buildings for the B&O Railroad. His first house designed on Mount Vernon Place was also for his patron Latrobe. With a fellow B&O draftsman James Crawford Neilson as his partner, their work on the Calvert and Franklin Street Station of the B&S Railroad was the greatest pre-Civil War railway station. Its "blockiness" followed the precepts he had learned at the Prague Polytechnik of primarily meeting a building's structural needs with its Italianate architectural style imposed secondarily rather than being foremost.

Other squares reminiscent of London such as Franklin Square had earlier been lined by the 1850s by row houses for the middle class in West Baltimore in the new Italianate style. These middle class houses were characterized by oval doorways, lintels over tall narrow windows and prominent roof cornices. The oldest of the six mid-century hilltop squares, Franklin Square contains one of the early homes of present day Coppin State University, now on North Avenue. The first black teacher training program was started there in 1900 as an outgrowth of the Douglass High School. It was named after Fannie Jackson Coppin, the first black female college graduate.

Other such albeit somewhat less fashionable squares that still encircle the heart of the city include especially Union and Lafayette Squares as oases in the otherwise formless and unplanned march of endless row houses. Union Square, named in a burst of patriotism, contains post-Civil War Italianate housing. The original estate house was deeded by a Carroll descendant to become a convent and school for delinquent girls that H.L.Mencken, an inhabitant of the square on Hollin Street, always found forbidding.

Landscaped boulevards such as North Broadway on the east and Eutaw Place with its dead end in Druid Hill Park along the western edge of Jones Falls were other attempts in the 1850s to bring the countryside into the city.

The omnibus first appeared on the streets of Baltimore in 1844. The use of rails starting in the 1850s enabled the horses to pull much heavier loads in a consistent fashion. The introduction of horse cars on the street railways in 1859 in Baltimore provided the beginnings of mass transit. Up to then, hackney cabs and private conveyances, beyond the reach of the average person, were the only alternatives to walking. A rather high fare of five cents was to be charged with one penny going to the city to support parks, one of which was the Druid Hill Park.

The Baltimore City Passenger Railway Company was the first and the most complete line. Others that later competed included the People's and Baltimore Traction as the most significant. Since several routes of the Baltimore City Passenger Railway Company used Baltimore Street, the various routes were distinguished by the color on their cars. For example, its Red Line (because of the color of its cars) started from Thames Street at Fells Point along South Broadway to the western end of Baltimore Street. Another line, first Blue then Green, ran from Baltimore Street up Greene Street and Pennsylvania Avenue to North Avenue; up Eutaw Street and Madison Avenue to North Avenue, at the boundary of the city. Druid Hill Park was the magnet. These latter lines ended one half mile below but were eventually permitted to go all the way to Druid Hill Park, the northern terminus.

The Druid Hill Park property is thought to have received its unusual name from its one-time owner Nicholas Rogers. He became familiar, while at the University of Glasgow, with the veneration the Druid priests had for hills with groves of oaks, so prominent on his estate. This centrally placed Druid Hill Park, funded with a tax on horse car receipts, was started in the 1860s to be filled with lakes, carriage drives and statuary. It was part of the same American public parks movement that led to the design of other urban parks simulating an English country landscape such as New York's Central Park and Fairmont Park in Philadelphia. After 1900, it also acquired athletic fields, swimming pools and playgrounds as an expression of the playground movement initiated in Baltimore by Robert Garrett, the grandson of John W Garrett, also one of the founders of the modern Olympic Games.

A radial city, the highways to the various points remain as first laid out around 1800 to be improved by private turnpikes. The important York Road leads north (used by the warlike Susquehannocks on their raids in the Chesapeake area), called Green Mount Road within the city boundaries. Reisterstown Road leads northwest to Hanover Pennsylvania, Frederick Road leads to Ellicott City and points west (later the National Road and US Rte 40) and Belair Road (Gay Street within the city) and Harford Road (Harford Avenue within the city) lead northeast to the county seat of Harford County (eventually to the Philadelphia Road) and Washington Boulevard runs southeast to Washington City. The last was the site of the ford used by the Native Americans crossing Gwynn's Ford near its mouth.

To stitch together the existing streets and create thoroughfares, jogs appeared or met in intersections of as many as five streets. A particular problem was streets crossing Jones Falls to integrate with the different pattern of Old Town. Street vistas ended in a house or a steeple or chimney rather than a site for a fountain or a park. Moreover, topography was ignored to the detriment of drainage with later requirements for costly filling, tunneling and bridging. However, the design made possible, like that of New York, the continuation of the process of subdividing land for speculative building.

The Poppleton Plan was preserved and extended for the area encompassed below North Avenue. It created a hierarchy of street widths with sixty-six feet wide avenues on the front and ten feet service alleys on the rear of the building lots. Lower status persons were socially and physically segregated to rear of the lots in the alleyways. Alley dwellings were not unique to Baltimore. They were a world-wide phenomenon in Great Britain as well as in many other cities in the United States. For example, the alley dwellings of Washington, inhabited mainly by blacks newly come to the city, created the same poor living conditions that existed in Baltimore. As population increased, so did the price of land and the intensification of population in what was still a "walking city," without easy cheap transportation for the working person. Blacks initially lived in the alleys in areas where whites might live on the front lots facing the street. In the 1870s, after the increase in black population that occurred because of the Civil War, the northward movement of better off whites into the higher ground, with horse car transportation now available, forced blacks into enclaves within white areas or into their own larger segregated residential areas.

The commerce of the city with the west via the National Road was being gradually superseded by the Mississippi and Ohio River system with the use of steamboats now enabling commerce upriver from New Orleans. Baltimore was also in competition with the Federal City and Philadelphia to funnel the trade of the Potomac and Susquehanna Rivers. Despite the opposition of Baltimore, the Maryland legislature committed itself to supporting the development of the Chesapeake & Ohio (C&O) Canal from the Ohio River along the Potomac River to Georgetown, and later to Alexandria as well as a canal along the Susquehanna. Instead, Baltimore committed to the wave of the future. A railroad was funded to the Ohio River Valley (B&O) and another to tap into the Susquehanna Valley (B&S) that would create the Baltimore of the later 19th century.

Robert Carey Long Jr was the Baltimore architect highly identified with the Gothic Revival ecclesiastical architecture that, emanating from Baltimore, especially characterized Catholic churches of the 19th century. He built in the 1840s the German Catholic St Alphonsus in the Gothic manner. The Gothic Revival pattern so established extended as far as St Mary's in Natchez Mississippi, commissioned by the former director of St Mary's Seminary in Baltimore. The Gothic Revival gatehouse by Robert Carey Long Jr at the main southeast corner of Green Mount Cemetery was the entry to Baltimore's romantic landscaped cemetery of the 1830s, analogous to Greenwood Cemetery in Brooklyn and Mount Auburn in Cambridge. The chapel by Niernsee and Nielson in the 1850s carried out the same mediaeval theme.

Born in 1810, Robert Carey Long Jr trained under his father, at Baltimore's St Mary's College before being apprenticed to the Connecticut-born Ithiel Town. One of the first generation of American professional architects, Town designed the Greek Revival Federal Hall in New York as well as the Egyptian Revival Wadsworh Atheneum in Hartford. Long carried out his Greek revival training with the Doric porch on the Lloyd Street Synagogue in 1845. The first established in Baltimore in 1830, its size reflected the substantial German Jewish immigration that had by now occurred. Reflecting still another source of immigration of the 1840s, Long's Irish

Catholic St Peter the Apostle Church near the large working class district adjoining Mount Clare B&O shops was also in the Greek revival fashion.

By the 1840s, the Roman Catholic Church in Maryland ceased to be the sole province of the Maryland aristocracy that had been its mainstay since its start in the 17th century. Like other port cities, the large immigration to Baltimore starting in the 1830s of Irish and particularly the non-English-speaking Germans caused the development of "national" parishes responsive to their language differences. The antagonism to this immigration was particularly evident in the "Know-Nothing" riots of the 1850s at election time consistent with the long history in Baltimore of riots since 1812. In the 1856 presidential election, Maryland was the only state carried by that party.

The antagonism to immigration expressed in the burning of the Ursuline convent in 1834 had been again short-lasting in the "American Republican Party" in the early 1840s. Anti-Catholicism was precipitated anew by the increased Irish immigration by the early 1850s by organizations such as the secret "Order of the Star Spangled Banner." There had also been the request for public funding of parochial schools and the prospect of a papal representative in the United States. In response, a defensive exclusively Catholic cultural unity arose that in turn excluded others, making Baltimore what it came to be in the last quarter of the 19th century.

During the first half of the 19th century, Baltimore continued to be the only archdiocese and the center of American Catholicism. As large Catholic populations appeared in the other port cities following the Irish Catholic immigration in the 1840s, in 1850 archdioceses were created in New York, Boston and Philadelphia. In recognition of that history, even when no longer the vital center of American Catholicism, the Archbishop of Baltimore retains the "Prerogative of Place," having precedence in councils in the hierarchy over all other American archbishops to the exclusion of any other's seniority of investiture or ordination.

2.2. Charles Willson Peale and the American Museum

Charles Willson Peale was born in 1741 in what was then Queen Anne's County in Chestertown Maryland. He was the son of a man transported to the colonies convicted as a felon after embezzling a large amount of money yet one who maintained a dignified air as a schoolmaster. Apprenticed to a saddle maker when aged thirteen, young Peale eventually became recognized as an artist. He was welcomed to Boston in the 1760s by John Singleton Copley. He received training in London under the American Benjamin West, sponsored in part by Charles Carroll "the Barrister." On his return, he worked in Maryland and Virginia as an artist-entrepreneur painting portraits with "a good likeness" of the planter and merchant elite in the style of his teacher Copley.

Fig. 14 - Charles Willson Peale

Unlike his fellow artists John Singleton Copley and Gilbert Stuart, Charles Willson Peale plunged into the American Revolution. His goal was to capture the faces and scenes of the Revolution for posterity. He came to Philadelphia in 1776 and joined the militia to fight in the Continental Army. He created a large number of heroic portraits of noteworthy early American figures with particular attention to George Washington. His full-length George Washington at Princeton commissioned by the Supreme Executive Council of Pennsylvania in 1779 is one of the best known among 60 different images.

The most essentially American of the first generation of artists that included Benjamin West, John Singleton Copley, and Gilbert Stuart; Peale spent only two years in Europe and worked almost entirely in the United States. He was dependent on local patronage primarily interested in portraiture rather than the fashionable history pictures that brought fame and fortune to his mentor Benjamin West. He did carry on West's focus on draftsmanship and clear lines in his portraiture that brought about the good likenesses that his subjects prized. His connections with the patriot cause stood him in good stead particularly in Maryland where from 1784 to 1793, he painted portraits of members of the Carroll, O'Donnell, Tilghman families and others of the Maryland elite.

Far more versatile than being merely an artist, Charles Willson Peale was a man of boundless energy. As a leader in the Whig Society, he engaged in politics including the writing of the relatively radical Pennsylvania State Constitution that contained a unicameral legislature. He invented such things as a "smokeless stove" still in place at Mount Clare, home of the "Barrister" as are his family portraits and the polygraph that was used extensively by Thomas Jefferson to make copies of his letters. Demonstrating a faith in America's commitment to high culture, he opened in 1802 in Philadelphia in the building of the American Philosophical Society America's first museum. It contained both his portraits of famous Americans and scientific specimens such as those collected during the Lewis and Clark Expedition as well as mastodon bones discovered in New York on an expedition under his own auspices. The latter reflected his interest in having a role in instructing rather than merely amusing the public and in his belief, after his mentor

Jean-Jacques Rousseau, that nature can instruct mankind. His museum's tickets read "The Birds and the Beasts will Teach Ye."

He connected a natural history museum together with an art gallery of famous personages, combining his artistry to his role of exalting the virtues of the new nation. Not only concerned with public instruction, he was also innovative in placing his specimens in settings reminiscent of their native habitats and in ensuring accuracy in the use of the Linnean nomenclature. However, his museum did not survive in that role of both public and scientific instruction. The collection was later acquired by P.T. Barnum for exhibit in a more sensational mode. Albeit short-lived, the Peale concept of a "museum" provided the model created by his son for a museum in the up and coming city of Baltimore.

Rembrandt Peale was the 3rd of his six living children of Charles Willson Peale from his first marriage and his major artistic successor. Born in 1778 in Bucks County Pennsylvania, he was trained mainly by his father but also studied in Paris and lived in London for a short time. His portraits were mainly of busts in the style of Gilbert Stuart unlike the full-length portraits done by his father. However, like his father, he painted many portraits of George Washington with the "Porthole Painting" one of the best known, now in the Old Senate Chamber of the U.S. Capitol. Also like his father, he opened a museum, but now in Baltimore.

In the first flush after Baltimore's great victory in 1814, Rembrandt Peale founded as an exemplar of a commitment to high culture the "Baltimore Museum and Gallery of the Fine Arts" on

Holliday Street. Designed by Robert Carey Long Sr, it was also the first building to be equipped with gas light, as a forerunner for the first street lights in the country to be placed outside his building. His brother Rubens Peale had witnessed the use of gaslight in London and had installed them in his father's museum in Philadelphia. This innovation was brought to Baltimore; the Baltimore Gas Light Company was organized to install street lights, the first in the United States.

In the absence of any model, the design of the building followed the pattern of important "English-style" houses of the period. The four small rooms on the ground floor with a large "drawing room" on the second floor were augmented by a very large double room on the rear for exhibits. The second floor drawing room was used for lectures; the rear room upper floor for the Peale portraits of famous Americans; the smaller rooms on the first floor for the displays of various natural history artifacts. Peale was also commissioned to paint portraits of the heroes of the recent Battle of Baltimore in 1814 that still hang in the Baltimore City Hall.

After 1822, Rembrandt returned to painting while his younger brother Rubens carried on the museum. The latter in turn added a live zoo as well as loan exhibitions of copies of "Old Masters." All the components of the "Universal Museum" were in place, to be accomplished eventually by the Smithsonian Institution but in Washington DC rather than in Baltimore. Closed in 1830, the building remains as evidence of an early forerunner of the eclectic museums devoted to public education and the more purely art museums that appeared in the generation after the Civil War.

After 1830, the building became the Baltimore City Hall, then after 1867 the No 1 Colored School. In 1928, it was rescued from destruction to become part of the Baltimore City Museum. On the garden wall is a sculpture done in 1808 by the Italians Giuseppe Franzoni and Giovanni Andrei of Ceres and Venus. They had been employed in the decoration of the U.S. Capitol under Benjamin Henry Latrobe but came to Baltimore for a short visit.

The flowering of Baltimore after its great victory in 1814 extended beyond the opening of the Peale museum to the formation of a literary club and magazine. Founded in 1816, *The Portico: a Magazine of Science and Literature* was an outgrowth of the Delphian Club. Its members included Francis Scott Key, John Pierpont and William Wirt as well as Rembrandt Peale. John Neal was the driving force behind the magazine as part of his prolific literary output. Born in Portland Maine in 1793, he came to Baltimore in 1816 and went into business for a short time with John Pierpont (the grandfather of J.P. Morgan). In a quest for creating an American literature independent of European influences, Neal helped produce 27 monthly issues from January 1816 to March 1818. With Baltimore seeking a role as the cultural center of the South, The *Portico* saw itself in opposition to the *North American Review*, America's first literary magazine established in Boston in 1815.

2.3. The Latrobe Family and the Building of Baltimore

Born in 1762 to an American mother in the Moravian Settlement in Yorkshire England, Benjamin Henry Latrobe was educated at a Moravian boarding school in Silesia before going on a European Grand Tour. Returning to England in 1784, he trained under the neo-classical architect Samuel Pepys Cockerell. The latter was responsible for the buildings of St George's Church in Hanover Square as well as some of the early squares in Bloomsbury and elsewhere in London's West End. Latrobe immigrated to Norfolk then Richmond in 1796 before moving to Philadelphia in 1798. He designed the Bank of Pennsylvania, the first Greek revival building in the United States. Complete with Ionic columns and pediment, it became the prototype of banks throughout the United States.

Well educated and well-travelled, Latrobe was the first professionally trained architect to work in America. He moved to Washington in 1806 to work on the U.S. Capitol. He sought simple shapes of cubes and spheres with classical details against plain surfaces, of models from ancient Athens. Finely fluted columns rose below vaulted brick ceilings; arched entrances led into domed vestibules. Ultimately, working with President Jefferson, he created in the Chamber of the House of Representatives the most sophisticated space in the entire country before its destruction by the British in August 1814; and rebuilt it afterwards.

Fig. 15 - Benjamin Henry Latrobe

After leaving the work on the U.S. Capitol, Latrobe moved to Baltimore in 1818 to complete the Basilica of the Assumption. Dying unexpectedly in 1820, his family remained in Baltimore to help create the 19th century city. His elder son John Hazlehurst Boneval (H.B.) Latrobe was born in 1803 while the family was living in Philadelphia. He was in training at West Point when called home after his father's death.

Trained in law, he became the major acquisition attorney for the B&O Railroad in its drive west. In addition, he was responsible for organizing Druid Hill Park and Green Mount Cemetery; the

Maryland Historical Society and the Maryland Institute of Art, the last one of the country's first. His son, Ferdinand Claiborne Latrobe (born 1833) was in turn seven times Baltimore's mayor intermittently from 1875 to 1895. His accomplishments included the improvement of the water supply to include the compounding of the water from Little Gunpowder River and the Montebello Reservoir.

The younger brother Benjamin Henry Latrobe II was born in Philadelphia in 1806 while his father was heavily involved in his work in Washington on the U.S. Capitol. Trained as an engineer, he served as the main construction engineer for the B&O Railroad, responsible for building many of the early stone arch bridges including the famous Thomas Viaduct on a curve crossing the Patapsco River between Relay and Elk Ridge on the Washington Branch of the B&O. His son, Charles Hazlehurst Latrobe (born 1833) worked with his father expanding the rail lines west of the Ohio River. He was appointed by his cousin when the latter was Baltimore's mayor in 1875 to be the chief engineer of the Jones Falls Commission. He built the containing walls and the early iron bridges crossing the falls at Calvert, Guilford and St Paul Streets as well as the iconic pagoda in Patterson Park.

Horse drawn omnibuses started in the 1840s to be replaced by horse drawn rail cars that connected the lower town with the residential areas uptown. Development occurred to the north to encompass the healthier and cooler higher elevation to go even beyond the 1816 Washington Monument. It had been established atop Charles Street carved out of Howard's Woods by the family of

John Eager Howard. One of the first memorials designed to honor George Washington, it was first proposed in 1809. Funded by a lottery, the Monument was designed by Robert Mills in 1815 with ground breaking on July 4th of that year. It continues to be the emblem of the soaring ambition of the city at that time.

Fig. 16 - Washington Monument

On a rectangular base containing a museum, an unadorned column rises in the model of Trajan in Rome and that of Napoleon in the Place Vendome. The column is the largest of its genre and considered one of the best proportioned. It is surmounted on a Doric base by a standing figure of George Washington by the Italian sculptor Enrico Causici, chosen by Mills. It is accompanied on the square by an equestrian statue of the young Marquis de Lafayette.

The architect Robert Mills was trained under Benjamin Henry Latrobe as well as being a protégé of Thomas Jefferson. Born in Charleston South Carolina, Mills was one of the pioneers of fireproof construction with the use of concrete. He was later also responsible for the design of the Washington National Monument in Washington DC as well as the Treasury Department, Old Patent Office and General Post Office, continuing the tradition of his mentors in creating a "museum of antiquity" in the national capital.

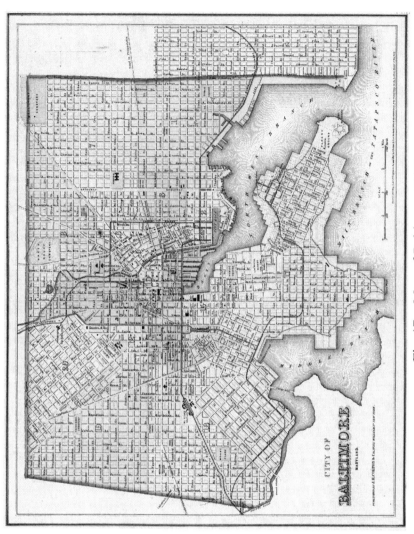

Fig. 17 – Map of Baltimore 1857

The adjoining map shows Baltimore in 1857 at its height of prosperity before the onset of the strife of the Civil War. Development had reached almost to North Avenue although the Druid Hill Park does not yet appear. Development of the industrial estate at Canton had occurred to the east of the city boundary. The B&O Mount Clare Yards were well developed on the west within the city boundary. The street system of South Baltimore adjoining Federal Hill had been laid out preparatory to the development of Locust Point.

During the era between 1820 and 1860, Baltimore grew by its water and road connections with the west. Its ample deep port was inland on the Chesapeake Bay to be secure from bad weather. The Susquehanna River directed trade from parts of central Pennsylvania and New York to Baltimore. Grain was grown in the Piedmont from Harford County all the way west to Frederick settled by hardworking mainly German farmers. Grain replaced tobacco as Maryland's main crop with coincidental reduction in the need for slaves to work the land. Agricultural practices improved such as the use of crop rotation and liberal use of guano fertilizer imported from Chile to Baltimore. Mills along the Fall Line converted the grain to flour along with the wood from the nearby forests converted to barrel staves and the schooners to take them to the customers in the West Indies. By 1843, the Baltimore & Ohio Railroad had also reached the coal and iron deposits of Cumberland Maryland on its way to the Ohio River to provide the basis for further industrial development.

2.4. George Peabody and the Mercantile City

The life and career of George Peabody exemplified the era in which Baltimore still competed successfully with New York and Philadelphia as a port city. George Peabody was born as one of eight children in a poor family in 1796 in what was then called South Danvers Massachusetts (now called Peabody after its favorite son). Leaving school after a sparse education that left him a lifelong poor speller, he was apprenticed at age eleven to a general store. The 1811 Newburyport Fire forced him to leave his native state.

On the eve of the declaration of war in 1812, he had started a small dry goods business with an uncle in Georgetown in the District of Columbia. In 1814, while serving for a short time in the Maryland militia, he met Elisha Riggs, a native of Brookeville Maryland, In 1817 Peabody, without capital of his own, entered the dry goods business in association with the more established Elisha Riggs, first in Georgetown and then in the larger thriving town of Baltimore.

The end of the War of 1812 opened up opportunities in foreign trade that had been disrupted by the Non-Intercourse Acts preceding the war. For the next twenty years, with Peabody the senior partner after 1829, his firm was headquartered in Baltimore. Peabody considered the city as his home even as he opened branches in New York and Philadelphia in association with other members of the Riggs family. George Peabody was the buyer with Samuel Riggs, the nephew of Elisha Riggs, now the junior partner responsible for sales. Most of their goods were sold from their own warehouse at their own store in Baltimore run personally by George Riggs. Acting on his own account, Peabody also sold on commission products to other markets throughout the world including New Orleans for the Mexican market and Lima Peru for the South American market.

Peabody first visited Britain in 1827 to negotiate the sale of American cotton to complement his purchase of finished goods for sale in the United States. His business in Liverpool was highly indentified with a branch of Baltimore's Alexander Brown & Company. Difficulties in using Baltimore as his main place for distribution arose because ships less frequently departed to Baltimore than to New York, which had regular weekly service. Travelling throughout Europe including France and Italy as well as the British Isles, his business grew with wider contacts while establishing a reputation for financial integrity. While several other firms failed, that reputation for financial integrity enabled his firm to receive credit enough from the Bank of England to weather the Panic of 1837 and helped save the Alexander Brown firm in Liverpool and Baltimore as well.

With the further advance in his reputation by his success during the 1837 crisis, he opened an office in London in 1838 that thenceforth became his base. The business of Peabody, Riggs and Company increased with its unusually good access to credit; its profits improved, enhanced by its size that guaranteed preferential treatment. In the 1840s, New York, long a serious rival to Baltimore's trade with the west, now began to have even more enhanced railroad connections. The use of steam ships enabled faster supply, again benefiting New York with its more frequent service. Increased domestic production of textiles affected the importation of British and European goods upon which the Peabody firm had been dependent. Baltimore's ability to compete as a port city began to recede as did the prosperity of even such large firms as Peabody, Riggs and Company.

Peabody founded his large fortune after leaving the mercantile firm. In the early 1840s at a time when American bonds, including those issued by the State of Maryland for the C&O Canal, were in default or disrepute, he bought the depreciated American bonds to sell later at a higher price. With the capital he had by now acquired, in 1847 Peabody withdrew completely from the dry goods business to become a merchant banker in London as "George Peabody and Company." He made the market for the sale of American securities in London as well as the sale of goods such as British iron for the building of American railroads in the 1850s.

One colleague was William W. Corcoran in Washington. The latter was in the banking business with George Washington Riggs, a son of Elisha Riggs. They also specialized in the selling of American securities to British investors including U.S. Government bonds and railroad securities. The first of the government loans guaranteed by the firm was at the time of the accession of John Tyler in 1844 after the very short presidential tenure of William Henry Harrison. They then financed the $15 million payment to Mexico in return for the cession of its territory after the end of the Mexican War. The placement of that loan with London bankers such as Baring Brothers in association with George Peabody was the start of a very profitable international banking business for all concerned.

In 1854, Junius Spencer Morgan (the son-in-law of John Pierpont and the father of J. Pierpont Morgan) entered the partnership, continuing the American and Baltimorean nature of the Peabody firm. The successor company headed by J. Pierpont Morgan remained the leading Anglo-American investment banker financing the 19th century industrialization of America. By this time in the 1850s, Peabody had already started his career as a philanthropist by supporting education in his native town. He became the founder of modern philanthropy in a model later followed by Johns Hopkins and Enoch Pratt in Baltimore as well as Andrew Carnegie and John D Rockefeller.

Peabody's philanthropy in England was devoted mainly to housing for the poor of London via the Peabody Trust. In the United States, Peabody, always cognizant of his own deprivation, endowed mainly educational institutions such as the Peabody School for Teachers at Vanderbilt University in Nashville Tennessee and the Peabody Institute in Baltimore, the latter eventually funded by $ 1.4 million.

Fig. 18 - George Peabody Statue

The Peabody Institute in Baltimore was founded in 1857 to include a free library, an art collection and a lecture series. It thus encompassed art; literature and music, a broad cultural base for the fast growing city previously without such a base. The art gallery was one of the first of its kind in the United States but its collection became absorbed during the Depression of the 1930s into the Walters Museum and the Baltimore Museum of Art; the Library became part of the Enoch Pratt and that of Johns Hopkins University. The still thriving music conservatory, now part of Johns

Hopkins University, is second in age in the United States only to the Oberlin Conservatory of Music.

Facing Mount Vernon Place, the west wing of the Peabody Institute, completed after the Civil War in 1866, is in an Italianate style containing the Peabody Concert Hall and an art gallery. The east wing containing the Peabody Library was completed in the 1870s. Called the "Stack Room," the outstanding interior with the glass covered iron work book galleries still exists. The architect Edmund George Lind was born in Islington London in 1829. After training as an architect at the London School of Design, he immigrated to the United States, eventually to Baltimore in 1855.

George Peabody was widely recognized for his philanthropy even before his death in 1869 by a seated bronze statue in front of the Royal Exchange in London. A replica, funded in 1890 by the Robert Garrett, then president of the B&O, was placed in front of the building of the Peabody Institute on East Mount Vernon Place. The sculptor William Wetmore Story was born in 1819 in Boston, the son of the Supreme Court Associate Justice and legal scholar Joseph Story. After graduating from Harvard College and Harvard Law School, he abandoned the law to move to Rome in 1850 to pursue a career in sculpture. His apartment in the Palazzo Barberini was the center for American expatriates living in Rome.

An English visitor in the 1850s credited Baltimore 'with the "intelligence of the north and the generosity of the south." Like the commercial cities of the North, Baltimore was dependent on foreign trade and manufacturing. However, like the agricultural states of the

South, Baltimore was the leading city of a border state founded on the cultivation of a staple crop like tobacco based on black slave labor. The manufacturers tended to support the Union, the landed gentry leaned toward secession; the latter were aided in their control of the state by archaic voter representation that denied Baltimore its proper voice.

Approximately 20% of the population of the state was foreign born or immigrants from other non-Southern states. By 1860, slaves represented a population of 87,000 out of a total state population of 687,000 with the majority concentrated in the tobacco-growing counties of Calvert, Charles, Prince George's, Anne Arundel, St Mary's and the Eastern Shore. Without any immigrant influx, the long term white population in these counties remained strongly Southern in its attitudes. The northern and western part of Maryland was populated by small holders with few slaves and little sympathy for slaveholders. Baltimore occupied an intermediate position in the state with its sympathies equally divided but with strong Unionist sympathy within the German immigrant community.

Due to the urban economic changes that made slaveholding less profitable, the city's slave population in 1860 had fallen to 2000 while its free black population had risen to 25,000, the largest in the nation but still encumbered by "black codes" that limited civil rights and economic opportunities. Illustrative was the life of Frederick Douglass who was born, probably in 1817, to a slave mother on a plantation in Talbot County on the Eastern Shore. As a boy of about ten, he was brought to Baltimore to live on Alliciana Street to serve as a companion to a white child, the son of a shipbuilder relative of his owner. Taught to read by his mistress despite the strictures of slaveholding, he never forgot the importance of education for creating his own sense of independence and freedom.

Moreover, living in the city, a slave like Douglass was much freer than those in a country plantation. Once taught to read, he could not be prevented from doing so and learning in a random newspaper about the work of the abolitionists. He gradually learned to write as well, if only to write his pass for freedom. Eventually in 1836, after an interval living as an agricultural laborer on the Eastern Shore, he returned to Baltimore to be rented out by his owner to be employed in a shipyard in Fells Point in Baltimore. Antagonism from white immigrant apprentices and carpenters competing for jobs drove him and other blacks out of their jobs. Despite this, he was enabled to work as a relatively well-paid caulker on his own with his earnings taken in large part by his owner. Having amassed enough money, he escaped to the North and freedom and a life as a leading spokesman for the abolition of slavery.

Fig. 19 - Young Frederick Douglass

2.5. Roger Taney and the Southern Interest

Baltimore was divided as was the state. However, the issue of fugitive slaves in the decade leading up to the Civil War, the right to secede, the role of the slave holding Border States during the war and the rights of the accused during the war all focused on Maryland and its native son of Chief Justice Roger Taney.

Fig. 20 - Roger Taney Monument

Roger Taney, born of a landowning family in Southern Maryland in 1777, moved to Frederick in 1801 after serving one term as Delegate to the Maryland Assembly from his home county and moved to Baltimore in 1823. A leading figure in Baltimore legal circles; he was, for example, one of the lawyers incorporating the Baltimore & Ohio Railroad in the late 1820s. Active in Federalist politics until the demise of the party, he deviated to the support of Andrew Jackson. Active then as the Maryland leader of the

Jacksonian party, he was appointed Chief Justice by Andrew Jackson in 1836 after serving as Jackson's Attorney-General and Secretary of the Treasury. In his latter role, he had acted on Jackson's behest vis a vis the Bank of the United States in the withdrawal of government funds.

Successor to the long time Chief Justice John Marshall, Taney was second only to his predecessor in his long tenure. Although at first a slaveholder, he had freed his slaves. He had argued successfully in favor of a minister who had preached anti-slavery to a camp meeting of several hundred Negroes. He had spoken with contempt of slavery and its ultimate demise. His attitude later hardened in favor of slavery by the time he wrote the majority opinion in the divisive Dred Scott decision in 1857 that dealt with the issue of citizenship as well as slavery. Taney's intemperate language contributed to the effect of the decision that was widely condemned in the North as an illegitimate use of judicial power to decide such a fundamental divisive issue.

Roger Taney remains recognized in Baltimore in bronze in the North Garden of Mount Vernon Place. Seated as though in the Supreme Court, he is draped in his judicial robes. It was designed in 1871 by William Henry Rinehart under the sponsorship of William T Walters. Born in Union Bridge Maryland in 1825, Rinehart was first a stone cutter before training under the patronage of Walters at the Maryland Institute of Art where his legacy supports the Rinehart School of Sculpture.

Slavery had been implicitly, if not explicitly, accepted in the Constitution by the 3/5 rule that guaranteed Southern power in the

House of Representatives and the Electoral College by counting as population their non-voting slaves. "Slave Power" maintained its ascendancy in national public life through its strength within the ruling Democratic Party supported not only by persons in the South but also many in the North. Business interests in the North closely allied with the South included the large New York City role in cotton brokerage and shipping.

Nearly a third of the population in 1790, by 1850 slaves comprised only one-sixth of the population of Maryland. Stimulated by the reversion of a tobacco economy to that of cereal production requiring far less labor, by the eve of the Civil War, there were approximately the same number of free blacks as there were slaves. This persisted despite a law requiring manumitted slaves to leave the state and the activity of colonization societies. Unlike other places at the time where large number of free blacks had a clear occupational role, the concurrent large number of unskilled whites prevented the development of a role in the larger economy. Rather the free blacks were an anomalous adjunct to the slave population. This was particularly evident in Baltimore with a large white immigrant working class competing for unskilled jobs with a relatively large number of free blacks.

The large number of free blacks coupled with the ease with which slaves could reach freedom in the neighboring state of Pennsylvania made the issue of fugitive slaves particularly prominent in Maryland. Although the actual number reaching freedom was far smaller than thought, it was still the largest of any slave state. Despite the Fugitive

Slave Act incorporated into the Compromise of 1850, efforts by Maryland slave holders to recapture their slaves in the adjoining Free States were hampered by the state courts as well as by opposition by the local population. Instead of the Dred Scott 1857 decision of the Supreme Court settling the issue, the decision caused a constitutional crisis that helped split the Democratic Party and precipitate the Civil War.

The slave Dred Scott sued for his freedom by having lived in several Free States while accompanying his Army medical officer owner on his assignments. In ruling against Scott, Justice Taney in 1857 went beyond the issue of freedom to deal with citizenship. He claimed that national rather than state law applied to citizenship. Thus, his decision appeared to deprive free blacks of the "due process" protection of the 5th Amendment offered by their status as native citizens of their several states. He ruled further that no black could be a "national" citizen unless he held citizenship at the time of the nation's founding. No black did so in 1776 or 1789. Since blacks could not be citizens, even as free blacks, they lacked the protections against the abuse of rights inherent in the implementation of the Fugitive Slave Law of 1850 that operated under national law. This also appeared contrary to the Constitution that provided for the rights established in one state to apply to other states. In several of the northern states, free blacks had been given citizenship merely by virtue of their birth. Thus after 1857, the implementation of the Fugitive Slave Act continued to be a source of continual court battles in the Free States.

In the context of the contested implementation of the Fugitive Slave Law as well as John Brown's raid, the sectional differences had become more prominent. The veneration of John Brown in the North as a martyr was inexplicable to the South fearful of a servile uprising that he sought to instigate. The national Democratic Party had now become more highly identified with the slavery interest of the South. The issue of slavery was paramount for the South led as it was by the large slave-holding planters, even if secession was not universally the means seen for its perpetuation.

The goal of the Southerners in the Senate such as Bayard of Delaware and Slidell of Louisiana was to throw the election of 1860 into the House of Representatives. The Democratic Party Convention was held in late April 1860 in the far from neutral ground of Charleston. Shock tactics prevailed. Despite strong Unionist sentiment even in South Carolina "to fight the battle within the Union," Alabama and then South Carolina led the withdrawal of the southern states from the convention. Radicals like Yancey of Alabama, Rhett of South Carolina and Ruffin of Virginia urged the break-up of the Democratic Party at the Charleston Convention. They saw that as a prelude to a Republican victory and secession. After 10 days of stand-off, the convention recessed.

The later Democratic Party convention in Baltimore in June 1860 did not heal the schism and nominated Stephen A. Douglas. A rump convention, also in Baltimore, attended by the Southern delegates who had left the Charleston meeting, then nominated John Breckinridge. They adhered to the pro-slavery platform defeated earlier in Charleston. A purely Southern ticket could not win with its potential of 120 electoral votes. (152 were necessary) but there was neither compromise on the platform by the Southerners nor any compromise on their candidate by the supporters of Stephen Douglas.

Three separate candidates thus ultimately vied for former Democratic votes with Stephen A Douglas of Illinois representing the old national Democratic Party; John C. Breckenridge of Kentucky, James Buchanan's Vice-President, the candidate of the Southern wing of the Democratic Party. Joseph Lane of Oregon was his vice-presidential candidate. A third group, "The Constitutional Unionists" with long-time member of Congress John Bell of Tennessee for President and Edward Everett of Massachusetts for Vice-President were a conservative combination of former Whigs and nativists with but one plank, preservation of the Union. All were united in opposition to Lincoln whose reputation was not only as being a "Black Republican" but as a backwoodsman and "non-gentleman." Although many in Maryland had manumitted their slaves, it was illustrative of the overall Southern character of Maryland that the result of the election in Maryland showed very few votes for Douglas or Lincoln. Evenly divided between the candidacies of John Bell of the Constitutional Union Party and Breckenridge of the Southern Democratic Party, the state's electoral votes narrowly went to the latter.

South Carolina was a hotbed of secession. Almost immediately after the November election, a convention was called. The convention, made up of many of the large planters, voted for secession on December 6, 1860. Conventions in the other Deep South cotton states in which the elite slave holders were also heavily represented, voted for secession during the month of January 1861. It is clear from the statements made by the delegates to the conventions voting for secession that the threat to the continued existence of slavery was the overriding concern. Although not as dependent on slaves, many in Maryland were sympathetic to the claim of states rights and that the Constitution was a compact of the states to which they had adhered and from which they could withdraw. However, the commercial connections of Baltimore extended not only to the south but also to the west and to the north and its loyalties were divided.

Fort Sumter became the key. On April 6th, Lincoln, in accordance with his Inaugural Address, decided to resupply but not reinforce Fort Sumter. On April 12th, Confederate batteries began to fire after Anderson had refused to evacuate the fort. The war had started but the crucial offensive action had been taken by the Confederates and the Union was to be defended. There would be no peaceful secession.

The secession of the upper South (Virginia, North Carolina, Arkansas and Tennessee) after the call for troops after Fort Sumter made even more important the final retention in the Union of the four Border Slave States. The retention of the Border States (Kentucky, Missouri, Maryland and Delaware) by the Union was crucial to the ultimate defeat of the Confederacy. They held significant work force as well as grain and other useful agricultural output. Moreover, they held much of the very limited industrial capacity of the South and exposed the remaining farms and shops of the Confederate war industry to much easier conquest.

Of all the Border States, Maryland was of course a special case. It surrounded Washington DC on three sides. The capital's only rail connection with the north was by the B&O line that ran from Baltimore. The B&O first came to Washington in 1835 via a line laid close by the long-time turnpike between Washington and Baltimore. The "Washington Branch" line left the main east-west line of the B&O at "Relay House" in Baltimore County named after the time when relays of horses were used to pull the cars along the tracks.

Maryland had not only voted for Breckinridge, the states-rights candidate; the state legislature was also pro-secession with its highly skewed rural composition. The vacillating but still stubbornly non-secessionist governor elected as a "Know-Nothing" refused to call the legislature into session for fear of a vote for secession. On April 19th, the 6th Massachusetts Regiment, the first fully equipped troops to respond to Lincoln's call after Fort Sumter, detrained to cross Baltimore on its way from the President Street Station of the Philadelphia, Wilmington & Baltimore line (PW&B) along Pratt Street to the Camden Street B&O train station to relieve Washington.

A riot on Pratt Street ensued with casualties on both sides, the first of the war. A secessionist rally took place the next day at the Washington Monument on Mount Vernon Place. The feelings stirred remain enshrined in a Confederate battle hymn, declared the state song of Maryland in 1939. "Thy despot's heel is on your shore,

Maryland...She spurns the Northern scum!" The Maryland authorities responded by destroying the bridges from the north of the Northern Central Railroad from Harrisburg while the mobs destroyed the bridge carrying the PW&B to its President Street station near Fells Point. Also destroyed were the telegraphic connections from the north to Washington. The capital was besieged, cut off from reinforcements and from any connection with the north.

Using the still intact PW&B line from Philadelphia to Perryville on the Susquehanna River, subsequent troop movements were able to bypass Baltimore. They used a ferry to join the Annapolis line of the B&O to enter Washington. Benjamin Butler, the Union commander of the 8th Massachusetts that followed the 6th Massachusetts, succeeded in taking this alternate route to the national capital via Annapolis. There was particular care that the ferry boat landing was on the federally-owned soil of the U.S. Naval Academy to allay Maryland's Southern sensibilities.

Finally, on April 25th, the 7th New York and the 8th Massachusetts marched down Pennsylvania Avenue to relieve the isolated capital city. Benjamin Butler occupied the Relay House in early May 1861 and, on his own initiative, occupied Baltimore itself a week later in mid-May with Federal troops encamped on Federal Hill. The city's supply of arms was removed to Fort McHenry. Baltimore remained under at least partial military occupation for the rest of the war and its leaders imprisoned for a time. On April 27th, President Lincoln had suspended the writ of habeas corpus in Maryland to "protect public safety." John Merryman, accused of participating in the destruction of the bridges, was imprisoned at Fort McHenry.

Now again, Roger Taney played a pivotal role in the Southern interest. The Chief Justice, sitting as the circuit judge for Maryland, ordered Merryman freed by issuing a writ of "habeas corpus." The Union commander refused to honor the writ in what became a cause célèbre. The battle between the Supreme Court and the Lincoln Administration was to be an ongoing one with Taney persistent in his opposition to the power of the presidency and Lincoln's use of what Taney deemed unconstitutional war powers.

Of a prominent Baltimorean family, Merryman's father had been a college classmate of Taney. Moreover, the issuance of such a writ, derived from the English common law, was one of the bulwarks of American liberty reaffirmed in the Judiciary Act of 1789. The writ was refused by the general in charge of Fort McHenry based on the existence of martial law in Maryland and the suspension of habeas corpus by the President. This had been done with great reluctance by President Lincoln when troops coming to relieve the city of Washington were being attacked in their transit though Baltimore.

Referring to the presence of the "suspension clause" as part of Article I of the U.S. Constitution, Taney denied the right of the President to act in the suspension of the right of habeas corpus without the agreement of Congress, not planned to be in session until July 1861. Taney's written opinion did not refer to the emergent nature of the situation and the President's possible "overriding responsibility to suppress rebellion" under Article II of the

Constitution. Taney remained steadfast throughout the war in opposition to the president, even in later cases based upon the Habeas Corpus Act of 1863, insisting that the continued existence of civil courts could exercise jurisdiction to the exclusion of a military court.

When the 37th Congress convened in special session in July 1861, Lincoln stated his overriding responsibility to suspend rights under his own reading of Article II of the Constitution and his oath of office. He did not, however, seek Congressional approval, the grounds of the Taney writ in the Merryman case. After rescinding in February 1862 the earlier suspension of habeas corpus and amnestying those arrested, Lincoln once again suspended that right in September 1862 This time, he subsequently sought and received Congressional approval in March 1863 in a Habeas Corpus Act. It freed the president to act but with restrictions and the reassertion by the Congress of its primacy in this regard.

Lincoln generally sought by constitutional means to bend the Court to his will. However, he never deviated from his position that necessity justified the exercise of arbitrary authority, ignored the procedures imposed by the Congress and chose to evade the Supreme Court having the opportunity to adjudicate his position. The Administration generally chose to evade test cases not only for issues of civil liberties but for other issues including the "Legal Tender Act" for fear that the court led by Chief Justice Taney would decide in the negative. Although prepared to issue such decisions on several occasions, Taney's poor health and eventual death prevented a further confrontation.

For example, the arrest and trial for treason before a military commission of Clement Vallandigham, a Democratic candidate for Ohio's Governor in 1863 once again appeared to offer a test case. The Court in turn evaded a confrontation. In 1864, it unanimously denied jurisdiction while Taney, unable to participate due to illness, had been ready to dissent based on the provisions of the Habeas Corpus Act of 1863.

Although the threat of a confrontation between the Executive and the Judiciary was evaded by both during the war, the "rule of law" was reinstated as soon as the war was over. The case of the civilian newspaper editor named Milligan was similar to that of Vallandigham. Sentenced to death by a military tribunal in Indiana, his sentence was confirmed by President Andrew Johnson in May 1865. The writ of habeas corpus was still denied but his execution was postponed. The case was finally considered by the Supreme Court in early 1866 after Taney had died, to be replaced by former Secretary of the Treasury Salmon P. Chase as Chief Justice. The Chase Court affirmed the right to review the actions of military tribunals in the case of civilians in the presence of functioning civilian courts, true in Indiana at the time. Thus, under the Habeas Corpus Act of 1863, the writ of habeas corpus was available to the accused. The stance by Taney re arbitrary arrests by the military in the presence of a functioning civil court system was thus supported once the war was over.

Maryland remained under Union control throughout the war. Contrary to expectations, the Maryland General Assembly did not endorse secession when it was finally permitted to meet. The Union Party gained control of the Assembly in the fall 1861 elections. However, the issue of slavery remained. Maryland, along with the other Border States, consistently refused the offer made by Lincoln in the spring of 1862 for compensated emancipation. However, the continuation of slavery became more problematic with the emancipation of the slaves in the District of Columbia in April 1862. Although Maryland was not officially subject to the Emancipation Proclamation issued in January 1863, the Fugitive Slave Law ceased to be enforced by the end of 1861. Despite the protestations of the Maryland Assembly, Union forces welcomed slaves as they fled into the District from neighboring Prince George's County. This became the basis for the large increase in black population in the District of Columbia that persisted after the war.

By 1863, slaves were being actively recruited in Maryland to join the Union army to meet draft quotas. Under the command of the son of a prominent abolitionist, a black regiment was being raised in Baltimore among the free blacks. In addition, freedom was promised to recruits as well as bounties and compensation offered to slave owners who had remained loyal to the Union. The market for slaves collapsed along with the power and authority of the slave owners. Under Unionist pressure, Maryland finally abolished slavery in its new state constitution of 1864, even prior to the passage of the 13th Amendment. However, once Union troops were removed after the war was over, the Democratic Party regained power and Maryland maintained its opposition to the spirit of both the 14th and 15th Amendments that sought to assure equal access to civil rights and to voting rights.

2.6. John Pendleton Kennedy and the "Middle Temperment"

Closely identified with Maryland life and politics during the antebellum era, John Pendleton Kennedy was born in Baltimore in 1795 the son of an Irish immigrant father and a mother from a wealthy colonial Virginian family. He was educated at Baltimore City College. His mother, living until 1854, was the dominant family figure that provided him with his southern legacy. It provided him with the attitude toward the benignity of slavery that suffused his early books in the 1830s.

Married to the daughter of a wealthy cotton mill owner, he was free to become one of the literary lights of Baltimore. After three well-received novels, he was readily compared with Washington Irving and James Fenimore Cooper as a basis for national literary glory. In addition to amassing what became the most extensive private library in Baltimore, he is credited with enabling Edgar Allen Poe's first publication. The major figure in an effort to create a cultural milieu in Baltimore, he also took an active role as president during the early development of the wide-ranging Peabody Institute.

His political career began in 1820 when elected to the Maryland House of Delegates. Although first elected as a member of the Democratic-Republican Party and supportive of Jackson in his first election in 1824, he eventually became closely associated with the anti-Jacksonian Whig Party in support of Henry Clay. His anonymous satirical political novel *Quodlibit* written during Jackson's second term was in the tradition of his Whiggish predecessors such as Joseph Addison and Richard Steele of the London *Spectator* and Jonathan Swift of *Gulliver's Travels*. This later writing also mimicked his early attempts at satire when he edited a magazine in 1819 called *The Red Book*.

Fig. 21 - John Pendleton Kennedy

The anti-Jacksonian novel satirized the formation of the Jacksonian "pet banks" and the hypocrisy dealing with their bankruptcy in the Panic of 1837. It seemed also to reflect his own repeated defeats at the hands of "democracy," and his long held conviction that an appeal to the masses was inherently dangerous although apparently necessary for victory. Elected to Congress as a

Whig on several occasions from 1838 onward, he was defeated when he opposed the annexation of Texas in 1844. One of his accomplishments while in Congress was the sponsorship of the bill funding the experiment to connect Baltimore and Washington by telegraph that carried messages along the B&O right of way. Secretary of the Navy in 1853 under Whig President Fillmore, he initiated several important naval expeditions including Matthew Perry's to Japan and Herndon's to the Amazon River. With the demise of the Whig Party in the 1850s, he refused to join either the "Know-Nothing" American Party or the Republican Party and withdrew from public life.

Associated with Baltimore's mercantile and industrial class rather than the planters, he came to view slavery as inefficient and unlikely to persist. As a Border State Unionist, he was opposed to secession but was also opposed to abolition as potentionally destructive of the Union. Based on his Whiggish distrust of popular politics and political parties, he considered the cries for disunion by Southern leaders as demagogues seeking merely personal gain. He similarly considered calls for abolition as"frenzy" to be brought under control by the presumably more thoughtful elite. Epitomizing his Border State "temperateness" between the two extremes, he found his home in the Constitutional Union Party in the 1860 presidential election. Under his auspices as the Maryland state chair, his party's candidature of John Bell and Edward Everett achieved a near majority vote in Maryland.

He remained influential in keeping Maryland out of the Confederacy in the crucial winter of 1861 when secessionists were on the offensive. He published in January 1861 his discourse on the role of the Border States where he pointed out that slavery was there in decline and that their interests were far more diverse than the "vast cotton field" of the Deep South. It was he who advised the wavering "Know Nothing" Governor Hicks to avoid calling the pro-secessionist House of Delegates into session. After the Baltimore Pratt Street riot in April 1861, he counseled Hicks to demand that Maryland militia troops called up be used only to defend the state and Union forces remain only on Federal territory, to calm secessionist agitation. However, in May 1861, he finally cast his lot and that of Maryland with the Union; and recognized the inherent conservatism of Lincoln's stance to maintain the Union, separate from emancipation.

He wrote a series of essays over the months starting in January 1863 published in the influential *National Intelligencer* newspaper that showed the evolution of his thinking. At first opposed to the Emancipation Proclamation, during 1864 he grew in his support of emancipation and Lincoln. By the end of the war, he became a Republican in favor of the 1864 Maryland Constitution that abolished slavery even prior to the 13th Amendment. He continued to support the political effects of emancipation despite the subsequent conservative 1867 Maryland Constitution created under the auspices of a resurgent Democratic Party. In 1868, he confirmed his new allegiance by introducing the nominees of the Republican Party in a large rally in Baltimore. He reaffirmed the pro-Union sentiments that had guided his political life and had helped maintain Maryland in the Union while also, in the spirit of the role he envisaged of the Border States, seeking reconciliation between the former warring sections.

CHAPTER 3
THE CIVIL WAR AND BEYOND 1865-1904

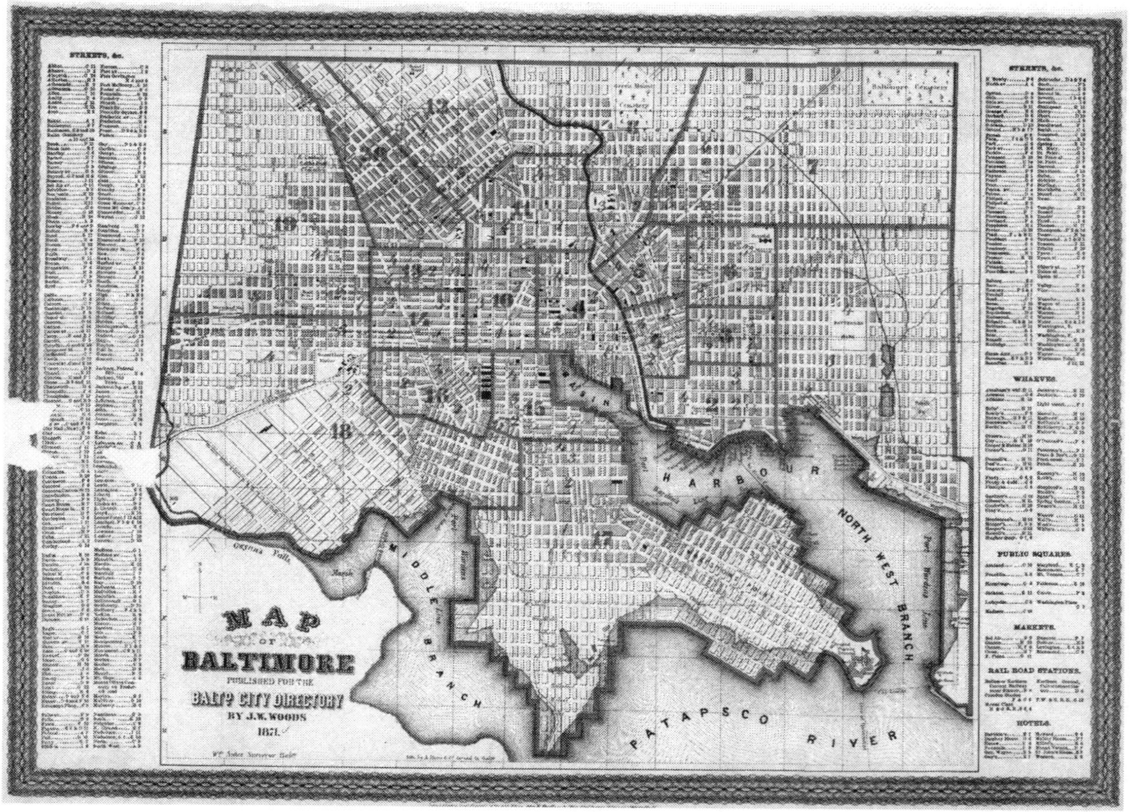

Fig. 22 – Map of Baltimore 1871

The adjoining map of Baltimore in 1871 shows the increased population during the period of post-Civil War prosperity of what had been laid out earlier as Canton and the more northerly the area of Highland Town surrounding an enlarged Patterson Park. Housing had also begun to fill in the area south of Federal Hill almost to Fort McHenry adjoining Locust Point. Development had moved west and particularly northwest toward Druid Hill Park yet the latter still does not appear within the city boundary that will extend north and west after 1888.

3.1. The Commercial/Industrial City/To Northern Parkway

The Erie Canal in 1825 gave the port of New York superior access to the west. The Chesapeake & Delaware Canal was Baltimore's answer to cut travel time for waterborne transport. Moreover, following 1828, Baltimoreans financed the first American railroad. Among its first directors were such familiar Baltimore names as Charles Carroll, William Patterson, Alexander Brown and Thomas Ellicott. With the start of service to Ellicott Mills in 1830, the Baltimore and Ohio (B&O) Railroad tracks reached Frederick in 1831, Harper's Ferry by 1834 and Cumberland Maryland by 1842.

The B&O left the Chesapeake and Ohio Canal permanently behind at Cumberland Maryland to reach the Ohio River at Wheeling in 1853. Baltimore with its railroad had clearly superseded the commercial ambitions of the City of Washington. The gauge of four feet eight and a half inches selected by the B&O based on the one mainly in use in England eventually became the standard for all American railroads The Carroll Viaduct built of stone over Gwynns Falls was the first American railroad bridge. Many of the innovations that made railroad travel efficient and safe originated with the B&O, built mainly by Irish immigrant workers who had come to Baltimore in the 1840s in the wake of the potato famine.

Peter Cooper from New York established an ironworks within Canton where he fabricated his "Tom Thumb" railroad steam engine, the first to compete successfully with horse power. A whole series of locomotives were developed that continually improved their efficiency and safety. By the 1850s, Baltimore was exporting locomotives to Europe. The equipping of the railroads provided buoyancy to the Baltimore economy to provide jobs to the native-born white artisans and the immigrants during the years leading to the Civil War with equivalent buoyancy in the building of the row houses.

The route of the B&O followed the Patapsco River to its source near Mount Airy and then west following the basin of the Monocacy River reaching the Potomac near Harper's Ferry. Eventually the B &O would connect to Cincinnati and St Louis despite differences in gauge of the various early segments and poor connections through the city of Cincinnati. Its "American Central Route," although closest to the west with its business boosted by a "freight rate differential", was the least efficient when compared with the less mountainous routes serving Philadelphia and New York. The competition between the B&O and the Pennsylvania Railroad headquartered in Philadelphia and extending through Pittsburgh was particularly intense but the other trunk lines of the Erie Railroad and the New York Central also competed strongly.

Even more controversial was the route to be followed into and through Baltimore to connect with the docks at Tidewater. There was a ridge of 140 feet at Mount Clare between Gwynns Falls and the Patapsco River. The City of Baltimore, one of the major stockholders, required the terminus to be at least sixty-six feet above tidewater, hence the Mount Clare station that favored west Baltimore on land donated by Charles Carroll "the Barrister," distant cousins of Charles Carroll "of Carrollton."

The "Barrister" branch originated in the United States with the arrival of Charles Carroll "the Chirurgeon" (surgeon) in 1715 from Ireland to Annapolis. Converted to the Anglican Church, Dr Carroll was free of the limitations that affected Catholics. He acquired the land along Gwynns Falls called "Georgia" in 1731. His son Charles, born in 1723, was widely educated at Eton, the University of Cambridge; and then studied law at the Middle Temple in London. Henceforth styled as "the Barrister," he was one of the wealthiest men in Maryland when he finally married Margaret Tilghman from Talbot County in 1763 thus marking an alliance with one of the leading families on the Eastern Shore commemorated in wedding portraits by his protégé James Willson Peale. Even before in 1756, he started building his summer retreat on his "Georgia Plantation." He ordered his limestone columns from Bath England. He called the still extant Federal house "Mount Clare" after the name of both his grandmother and sister. The greenhouse contained not only orange and lemon trees but a "pinery" containing the even more exotic pineapple plants.

Despite the wishes of James Maccubbin Carroll, the nephew and heir of the Barrister, who donated to the B&O the right of way across Gwynns Falls, the railroad did not reach tidewater at Carroll Point just south of Mount Clare. Eventually in 1853, the B&O connected to the level of the port at their new Camden Station, displacing the black community then living there.

The Baltimore & Susquehanna (B&S) on its way to York Pennsylvania was similarly placed at a height of ninety feet above tidewater at the then northern city boundary of Calvert and Franklin Streets. It remained cut off from the tidewater until tracks could be snaked through to reach Fells Point. Running circuitously along the valleys of streams such as Jones Falls; and then Gunpowder Falls on the way to Harrisburg, it was eventually taken over in the 1850s as the Northern Central line. Thus allied with the Pennsylvania Railroad, the Northern Central would be connected by the "Union" Railroad tunnel to Canton on the harbor at the President Street Station. Its access to the anthracite coal fields of Pennsylvania brought heating coal to Baltimore at low prices.

The Philadelphia, Wilmington and Baltimore (PW&B) had already built its terminal at President Street in the Canton area to the southeast to become later a part of the "Union Station" of the Pennsylvania Railroad. All these facilities to the benefit of the stockholders of the Pennsylvania Railroad were taxed at a low to non-existent rate by the City of Baltimore.

At the start of the Civil War, after having taken charge of opening the route to besieged Washington, by August, 1861 Thomas Scott, a vice-president of the Pennsylvania Railroad, was appointed Assistant Secretary of War by Secretary Cameron (himself a director of the Northern Central Railroad allied with the Pennsylvania). Appointed to be in charge of the railroads serving Washington, Scott remained in his position through June 1862 to the great profit of the Pennsylvania Railroad. It charged standard rates for military transport that made the government railroad traffic highly lucrative. Cameron was soon deposed and Secretary of War Edwin Stanton appointed in January 1862. The latter was a friend of the competing B&O and its president John Garrett, having been general counsel of the Ohio Central Railroad when it was being merged into the B&O.

In 1860, Baltimore was still mainly a mercantile city dependent on trade with western and southern markets with an extensive international trade, particularly with South America. Production was mainly still by artisans living close by to the central wharves and warehouses related to such trade who were able to walk to work. This southern mercantile trade was cancelled by the war; and not re-established until long after its end. The Mount Clare Yard of the B&O, devoted to the maintenance of the railroad throughout the war, was a major source of employment. Aside from the B&O Railroad railway repair yards adjoining Mount Clare with their Irish workers living nearby; to the west of the central district, large clothiers and shoe manufacturing predominated. In general, larger steam driven industrial establishments had begun to proliferate in this area.

To the east of the central business district along Baltimore Street artisan-type establishments continued to exist. These smaller establishments continued to include a place for production, sales and residence and where "putting out" production by unskilled women and children in their homes also continued. Further to the east in Old Town were the breweries and food processing plants. Shipbuilding remained the dominant industry at Fells Point where the labor force increasingly made up of mainly Irish and German immigrants was busy during the Civil War. Other cities less vulnerable in their position between the North and the South such as Pittsburgh as well as the more northerly port cities gained much more than Baltimore from expenditures in support of the war effort.

Primarily a commercial city, Baltimore continued to lag behind in its industrial development and lost its place behind New York, Philadelphia and other growing cities such as Pittsburgh and Chicago. Moreover, its industrial employment tended to be highly seasonal interrupted even more by recurrent depressions. A low-wage town, wages remained depressed by the presence of a large number of white immigrants and by blacks, both available as strike breakers.

3.2. John W. Garrett and the B&O Railroad

Fig. 23 - John W. Garrett

On the eve of the war, the Garrett interests, including Johns Hopkins as one of his associates and major stockholder, took control of the B&O Railroad in a stockholder revolt. The B&O had ceased paying dividends embarrassed as it was by heavy indebtedness incurred by the drive to reach the Ohio River at both Parkersburg and Wheeling.

During the Civil War, Garrett managed to maintain the oft-attacked B&O's main line despite major depredations. There were long interruptions in 1861 and 1862 and recurrent shorter interruptions due to lesser guerilla raids through 1864. Among its accomplishments, the railroad contributed to the transfer of troops for the Battle at Gettysburg in June-July 1863. In addition, the B&O

was able to transport the troops under General Lew Wallace from Baltimore to the Battle of Monocacy in July 1864 to forestall Jubal Early from his attack on Washington for one crucial day. In addition, the formation of the breakaway state of West Virginia during the Civil War in 1863 provided a personal Garrett fiefdom of coal and timber.

The Washington Branch connecting Baltimore to the south remained in uninterrupted operation throughout the war with more than a tripling of freight revenue and more than a quadrupling of the even larger passenger revenue. The huge increase in freight led to the building of additional side rails. A double line was eventually laid from Relay House to Bladensburg near the District line in 1864. However, the heavily-travelled passenger route between Washington and New York included at least three separate railroads. The B&O operated the only line between Baltimore and Washington; the Philadelphia, Wilmington & Baltimore continued to Philadelphia via a ferry over the Susquehanna between Havre de Grace and Perryville; the Camden & Amboy ran through New Jersey to the Raritan River and then via ferry to Staten Island.

John Work Garrett was the second son of Robert Garrett I, a Scotch-Irish farm boy who moved from Washington County Pennsylvania to Baltimore in 1820. Robert Garrett I's father had been the youngest of seven children born in Northern Ireland. Robert Garrett I established a prosperous produce and commission house based on the western trade carried by Conestoga wagons on the National Road.

Born in 1820, John W. Garrett joined his father and elder brother in their business. Increasingly prosperous as agents of George Peabody and Company in London, both brothers bought shares in the B&O and were members of its board that gained control in 1858. Initially unfamiliar with the railroad business, Garrett was firmly in charge during the difficult civil war years. He was re-elected president of the railroad for a total of twenty-six years until his death in 1884. His home on Mount Vernon Place was augmented in 1870 by the estate farther north called Montebello formerly owned by Samuel Smith. Inherited by his daughter Mary Elizabeth Garrett, it served for a time as an adjunct to her Bryn Mawr School.

Under John W. Garrett, the B&O reached an agreement in the 1860s with the North German Lloyd shipping firm that brought a large number of immigrants to Locust Point to be shipped west; the road finally reached Pittsburgh in 1871 to break the monopoly of the Pennsylvania Railroad to that important city; and reached Chicago in 1874. Garrett maintained as high as a 10% dividend on B&O stock while cutting wages during the long depression that followed the Panic of 1873. In July 1877, the railway men struck by taking control of the railroad yard in Martinsburg, ending only after the use of federal troops. Ultimately, particularly under his son and successor, the B&O established a system that provided greater benefits for their employees that reduced tension.

At that same time, the old Washington Branch line south from Baltimore at Relay House was supplemented by the more direct Metropolitan Branch line that ran northwest from Washington to join the main B&O line going west at Harper's Ferry. Long delayed, it was contrary to the B&O's original and still primary goal of enhancing the role of Baltimore to the detriment of Georgetown and Alexandria. Moreover, the rival Chesapeake & Ohio railroad (C&O) competed for the extensive coal traffic generated in West Virginia; the Baltimore & Potomac (B&P) of the Pennsylvania Railroad competed on the coastal route to Washington DC with a rival station near the U.S. Capitol on the National Mall.

Refusing to dilute the stock ownership, Garrett financed the expansion of his railroad line by taking on debt. The B&O's loans were sold in the London market by the Morgan firm, the successor of the original Baltimore-based George Peabody and Company. By the time of his death in the 1880s, the B&O system, buttressed by its rate differential by the shorter distances from Baltimore to the Mid-West, had tripled its mileage since 1865 to extend over 1700 miles. Its impressive headquarters was at the important corner of Baltimore and Calvert Streets. However, it lagged in investment in improving the railroad in competition with the Pennsylvania Railroad. In the 20th century, the B&O came for a time under the domination of its rival before undergoing a series of mergers and acquisitions and refinancing to the eventual detriment of the future of Baltimore as its headquarters town.

The Garrett family continued to affect Baltimore. The family of his second son T. Harrison Garrett remained connected with Evergreen House bought in 1878. First an Italianate country house designed by Niernsee and Nielson in the 1850s, it became a much more ornate neo-classical mansion complete with a Corinthian columned portico and Italian gardens, Tiffany glass canopy, art gallery and theater with sets by Leon Bakst. Its extensive library remains the rare book depository of Johns Hopkins University.

Even more far reaching was the life of Mary Elizabeth Garrett, the only daughter. An intelligent and restless woman, she declined to live the life assigned to her by her class and gender. Together with her close friend M. Carey Thomas, one of the first women to earn a Ph.D., they founded the Bryn Mawr School for Girls and Bryn Mawr College. She also helped build the Johns Hopkins School of Medicine to complement the already ongoing Johns Hopkins Hospital. The fund raising effort by the national Women's Medical Fund led by her and M. Carey Thomas in Baltimore required an agreement of the Hopkins trustees to admit women "on the same terms as men." Active in the feminist movement, she succeeded in making it socially acceptable for women of her class in Baltimore.

3.3. Johns Hopkins and American Medicine

The benefactions of Johns Hopkins also arose out of the success of the B&O Railroad. They continue to have impact not only on Baltimore but on the entire world. Constrained by his will not to sell the B&O stock, the university later suffered from the difficulties that beset the railroad.

Fig. 24 - Johns Hopkins

Johns Hopkins was born in 1795 of Quaker parents on a tobacco plantation in Anne Arundel County just south of Baltimore. The second of eleven children, he left school at age twelve in 1807 to work on the plantation when his devoutly Quaker parents freed their slaves. He remained an abolitionist and a supporter of black rights the rest of his life. Moving to Baltimore, he joined his uncle Gerard Hopkins's commission business. In business on his own with his brothers, Hopkins prospered selling goods in Virginia's Shenandoah Valley with the whisky frequently taken in exchange called "Hopkins Best."

A stockholder and then board member of the B&O, he chaired its finance committee and teamed with John W Garrett in the latter's takeover of the company, The largest single individual stockholder with 15,000 shares at the time of his death, the never married Hopkins had a well-deserved reputation of parsimony. He nevertheless used his wealth in the spirit of George Peabody to endow a great institution. An actual meeting between the two men under the auspices of John W Garrett might have taken place. In the fall of 1866 when Peabody visited Baltimore, he is thought by some to have provided Hopkins with the concept of establishing his endowment but not necessarily, the direction it would take.

At his death in the early 1870s, Hopkins bequeathed $3.5 million, then an enormous sum, to found his university that eventually became, on the German model, a graduate school that was the first in the United States to issue a Ph.D. This benefaction, derived from the commercial success of Baltimore and its railroad, created a great university at a time when the City of Washington could not generate the wealth to support an equivalent. Moreover, an equal amount was bequeathed to found the Johns Hopkins Hospital as the forerunner of the Johns Hopkins Medical School. At a time when the B&O stock bequeathed by Hopkins was no longer generating dividends, the building of the medical school was largely funded by Mary Elizabeth Garrett with the proviso that women would be admitted on a basis equal to men.

The still extant domed hospital building at Orleans Street and Broadway, the former site of the Maryland State Mental Asylum, was first designed by John Rudolph Niernsee, the leading Baltimore architect of his time. Separate distribution of heat and ventilation to each of the wards to reduce cross contamination was designed to prevent spread of infection. The final design attributed to John Shaw Billings, the building carries his name. Before being called to the new Johns Hopkins Hospital, John Shaw Billings headed the Library of the Office of the Surgeon General. He created there *The Catalogue of the Library of the Surgeon General* and the long lasting *Index Medicus*.

The John Hopkins Medical Institution was the leader in creating a strong connection between clinical medicine and scientific research that became the model that created modern American medicine. What was particularly innovative was that the hospital was under the control of the medical school at a time when the opposite was more common. Sir William Osler speaking in 1918 on the evolution of American medicine placed it in the context of its predecessors such as French medicine from 1820 to 1860 and German advances from 1860 to 1890. He considered the decision to place the hospital within the university as initiated by Johns Hopkins to be an important cause of the rise of American medicine to first rank.

3.4. The Johns Hopkins Hospital Faculty

The early leadership of William Welch set the tone for the development of Johns Hopkins to first rank. Appointed in 1885 by the Hospital Director John Shaw Billings, Welch espoused the principle of the connection of the study of pathology after death on the treatment of disease in life. Born in 1850 in Norfolk Connecticut, he was the son of a long line of physicians. He studied the classics at Yale and taught Greek and Latin after graduation. His education at the College of Physicians and Surgeons at Columbia was followed by training in pathology at Bellevue Hospital. He then travelled abroad in the tradition of 19th century American medical students. At a time when German medicine was the best in the world, his teachers included von Recklinghausen in Strasburg, Julius Cohnheim in Breslau and Carl Ludwig in Leipzig.

Fig. 25 - William Welch

When appointed to Johns Hopkins, Welch was one of the most broadly trained scientists of his day. His research focus was infectious disease with the isolation of *Clostridium welchi*, the cause of gas gangrene, one of his discoveries. His research ceased after the formation of the medical school when he became devoted to medical education and administration. After retirement from the medical school in 1916, supported by the Rockefeller Foundation, he founded the Johns Hopkins School of Hygiene and Pubic Health; and medical schools staffed by Hopkins-trained physicians established by Rockefeller were established to bring the benefits of Western medicine to China. In 1927, Welch established the Institute for the

History of Medicine and its Library, the first of its scope in the United States in time to receive European scholars fleeing Nazism. The elder statesman of American medicine, his 80th birthday in 1930 was addressed by then President Hoover.

Welch's most direct influence on medical education was his selection of the rest of the great initial Hopkins faculty. The most famous was William Osler recruited from the University of Pennsylvania Hospital in Philadelphia to become Chief of Medicine. Osler raised to a high art his format of lecturing to small groups of students at the bedside based upon the clinical manifestations of the patient. He also initiated the involvement of medical students with patients on the wards that became known as the clinical clerkship for senior students. He was enthusiastic in welcoming medical students on his ward rounds and delighted in teaching. Many years later, former medical students recalled his warmth in encouraging them to be bibliophiles with particular interest in Sir Thomas Browne and his book *Religio Medici* that speaks of his moral and spiritual life as a physician in 17th century England.

Fig.26 - Sir William Osler

Born in 1849 in what was then known as Canada West, his father was an itinerant Anglican minister. Osler eventually trained in medicine at McGill University in Montreal. After graduation in 1872, he returned there in 1874 as Professor of Medicine before appointment to the University of Pennsylvania. After appointment as Physician-in-Chief at Johns Hopkins Hospital in 1889, he remained as Professor of Medicine at the Johns Hopkins Medical School until 1905 when he became Regius Professor of Medicine at Oxford and later received a baronetcy. He instituted the format of the long term medical residency and specialty training that still characterizes American medicine. Successive editions of his book *The Principles and*

Practice of Medicine was the standard text for generations of students from its first publication in the 1890s.

Fig. 27 - William Halsted

Another of the great men of the first Hopkins faculty was the Chief of Surgery William Stewart Halsted. Born in New York City in 1852, he was educated privately and then at Phillips' Academy Andover before going to Yale and Columbia College of Physicians and Surgeons in 1874. He met William Welch while working in New York and then studied in Europe under the great men of the Viennese School of Medicine. Returning to New York in 1880, he began an exciting and innovative surgical career. He is credited with carrying out the first gall bladder operation and the first use of blood transfusion.

Experimenting with the newly discovered use of cocaine as a local anesthetic, he remained addicted to it and later morphine when the latter was used as a vehicle for curing the addiction to the former. With the support of his friend William Welch, he was nonetheless able to carry on his career as one of the leading surgeons of his day. He founded at Johns Hopkins the first surgical residency program, defined the techniques for aseptic surgery and created many of the operations such as that for breast cancer that remained current for the generations that followed.

Aside from the Medical School and the Hospital, the Johns Hopkins University developed from the plans of its president Daniel Coit Gilman. Born in Norwich Connecticut, he trained at Yale then Harvard before study in Europe. He joined the faculty of the Yale Sheffield School in political geography before starting up the University of California in Berkeley. He is credited with the concept of a university primarily devoted to graduate studies leading to a doctorate. With the primary focus being faculty, the first buildings were nondescript at North Howard and Centre Streets near the Peabody Library upon which its students could draw. Johns Hopkins University Press was the first of its kind, founded to publish the work of its faculty. The initial plan to use the Hopkins estate at Clifton as the university campus changed around 1900; the extensive gardens and Italianate house became Clifton Park while the Hopkins campus arose in Wyman Park near Homewood.

3.5. Henry Walters and the Walters Art Gallery

The early bevy of Baltimore philanthropists continued with the creation of a world class art collection, albeit long after other cities. William Thompson Walters was born in Pennsylvania somewhat north of Harrisburg in 1820, his father the leading banker in

Harrisburg. He trained as a civil engineer in Philadelphia and worked in the anthracite and iron industry in places such as Pottstown. He came to Baltimore in 1841 in conjunction with the completion of the tidewater canal on the Susquehanna to Havre de Grace and then to Baltimore. He entered the produce and, after 1850, the liquor business as W.T. Walters & Company. The firm's warehouse dominated Lombard Street until the Great Fire of 1904.

He was first involved in the 1850s with the Northern Central Railroad that brought coal from the Pennsylvania fields. A controlling director of the forerunning Baltimore and Susquehanna (B&S) Railroad, he increased his holdings in railroads devastated by the Civil War that served Virginia and the Carolinas where his produce business also lay. Eventually, he organized the Atlantic Coast Line Railroad between Wilmington North Carolina and Washington, the foundation of his fortune.

Living in exile in Paris during the Civil War due to Southern sympathies, he began actively to collect the work of then contemporary artists such as Millet, Delacroix, Daumier and especially the sculptor Antoine Louis Barye. The last, born in Paris in 1796, trained as a goldsmith before entering L'Ecole des Beaux-Arts at its start in 1818. In association with his friend Eugene Delacroix, Barye would sketch the way animals moved in the Zoological Gardens. At the height of his career in the late 1850s, he was famous as a sculptor in bronze of both small and increasingly larger pieces that included animals in association with classical themes. A sculpture like *Theseus and the Minotaur* is illustrative of his work. Sponsored by

William Walters, along with the *Seated Lion*, his less common non-animal sculptures called *Peace, War, Order and Force* stand in Mount Vernon Place across from the Walters Museum of Art.

Fig. 28 - William T Walters

Having returned to Baltimore with his treasure installed in his town house on Mount Vernon Place, William Walters opened it to the public on selected days. His collection of Chinese Imperial porcelains received a special room. His son Henry shared his father's devotion to business and to art. He augmented the Atlantic Seaboard Coast line with the parallel long-established north-south Louisville and Nashville (L&N) Line. Reputedly the richest man south of the Mason Dixon line, Henry Walters expanded the breath and depth of the collection to include not only works by Ingres and by such impressionists as Monet and Cassat but works of Raphael and El Greco. A major coup was the purchase in 1900 of the entire collection of the Palazzo Accoramboni in Rome including its ancient archeological treasures.

Although living mainly in New York and heavily involved with the Metropolitan Museum of Art, Henry Walters left to the people of Baltimore his wide ranging collection and an Italian palazzo to house it on Mount Vernon Place. Baltimore finally had a museum of high art comparable to that of Boston and New York.

The business of Baltimore was as "The Gateway to the South." In the Reconstruction era, it alone had the long standing commercial connections that enabled merchants to choose more wisely those to provide with credit. Among those commission merchants were men such as Enoch Pratt. In a story by now familiar, similar to that of George Peabody and Johns Hopkins, Enoch Pratt was another of the Baltimore philanthropists of the mercantile city.

3.6. Enoch Pratt and the American Library

Fig. 29 - Enoch Pratt

Born in 1808 in Middleborough Massachusetts and educated at the Bridgewater Academy, he came to Baltimore in 1831. Established in the hardware business, he thrived while shodding the Union horses and mules of the Civil War. He was also an investor and officer of the Philadelphia, Wilmington & Baltimore Railroad, eventually absorbed in the Pennsylvania Railroad as the main road to the North as well as the owner of the "Bay Line" that ran ships to Norfolk. Along with William Walters, Pratt was one of the founders of the Safe Deposit and Trust Company. His Mercantile Trust Company was Baltimore's 3rd largest. A New Englander, he was both a Union supporter and the mainstay of the Unitarian Church. Unlike his contemporary and also childless Johns Hopkins, he married and was a far more expansive personality. He lived at Park and Monument Streets, now the home of the Maryland Historical Society.

In addition to the funding of the Sheppard Asylum as the Sheppard and Enoch Pratt Hospital for the Mentally Ill, he supported the Colored Boys Orphans Home along with his fellow philanthropist Johns Hopkins. His most significant legacy is the Enoch Pratt Free Library. His gift included not only the central library but an extensive and innovative branch library system and horse drawn mobile libraries open to all regardless of color. In a model apparently explicitly followed by his friend and fellow iron-maker Andrew Carnegie in his own funding of free libraries, Pratt would ordinarily provide the buildings but required the city to commit funds for their ongoing support.

Libraries in Baltimore followed the pattern elsewhere. Early libraries were private and usually small. One of the largest in Baltimore was that of John Pendleton Kennedy with over 5000 wide-ranging titles. Kennedy was a lawyer and politician as well as a writer. He was active in all the cultural activities including the Baltimore Library Company, in imitation of the one founded in Philadelphia by Benjamin Franklin. Founded in 1795 and led by Archbishop John Carroll until 1815, this elite company lasted until 1856 when it merged into the library of the Maryland Historical Society. The more popular Mercantile Library Association was founded in 1834 by John H.B. Latrobe to serve a more middle class clientele. It too joined with the Baltimore Library Company and the Maryland Historical Society in an Atheneum built in 1848 at Saratoga and St Paul Streets.

The founders sought a public subscription for their new building in 1848 since "Baltimore should blush as being the only major city without a 'temple for literature and science'." This building replaced the original Atheneum from 1824 at St Paul and Lexington Streets founded mainly by several men who were New Englanders and Unitarians in the spirit of their native city of Boston. This effort was part of a broader effort by these same men to replicate some of the other reforms initiated in Boston including public schools. The Atheneum building that burned down in 1835 also contained as an example of these new educational initiatives the first classes of the Maryland Institute for the Promotion of Mechanical Arts, later the Maryland Institute College of Art. It was also most notably the site of the 1832 conventions that nominated Andrew Jackson and Henry Clay for their respective party tickets.

A four-story Italianate building designed by Robert Carey Long Jr, the 1848 Atheneum incorporated the several private libraries as well as the home of the Maryland Historical Society. Unusual for its time, it also incorporated an art gallery. It thus served as a predecessor to the multiple functions of the Peabody Institute that fulfilled the original goals proposed by John Pendleton Kennedy in the 1840s for a library, art gallery and lecture hall. The Maryland Historical Society moved to its present location at West Monument Street in 1919 where its collection strongly reflects the success of Charles Willson Peale in painting the Maryland planter elite.

CHAPTER 4
THE IMMIGRANT CITY 1904-1945

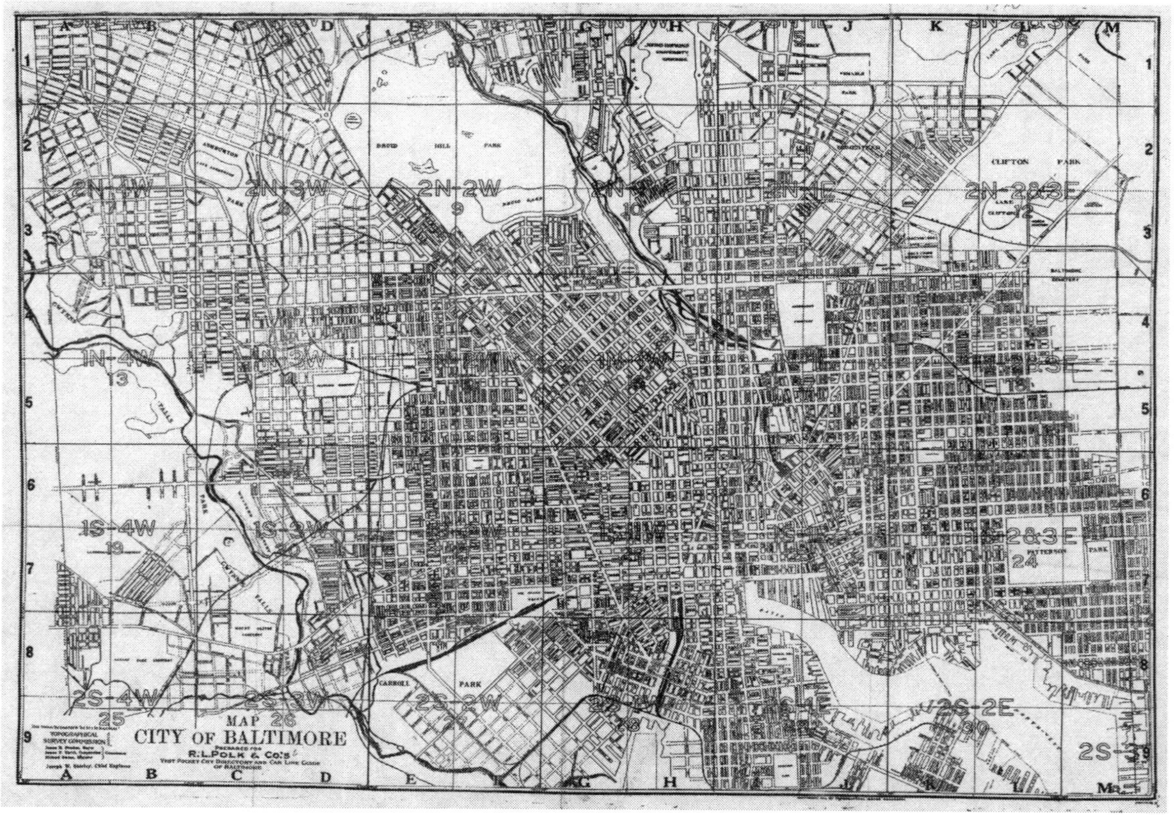

Fig. 30 - Baltimore 1910

4.1. The Industrial City /To the County Line

The adjoining map of Baltimore in 1910 shows the development that occurred following the Great Fire of 1904. Druid Hill Park is an integral part of the city. Mapping of streets had extended northwest to include Forest Park and Lake Ashburton opened in 1910. Carroll Park had appeared in the southwest. To the east, development was approaching Clifton Park. Lake Montebello had been delineated as part of the water supply system. The Johns Hopkins campus was delineated on Charles Street. The railroad stations had been established at Mount Royal and Camden Stations for the B&O; and for the competing North Central and the Pennsylvania Railroad on North Avenue.

The opening of the Panama Canal increased the value of Baltimore as the closest port-of-call supplemented by its shorter distance to the mid-West by rail. Although less true than for many other of the cities in the North and Mid-West, far more than any of the cities of the South, Baltimore was also increasingly an industrial city. By 1873, there were large factories that manufactured clothing and shoes. By 1880, 26% of those employed were engaged in manufacturing whereas only 7% were so employed in any other Southern city.

Canneries were particularly important as large scale employers in Fells Point. Starting with oysters, canning became Baltimore's second largest employer with canning of fruits and vegetables filling in during the summer months. Mainly women and children, the cannery workers were at first German immigrants, to be succeeded by Poles. In 1879, reflecting the large Polish population near their place of work, St Stanislaus Kostka Church was founded in Fells Point, the first of several "national" Polish parishes in East Baltimore.

Replacing after 1868 the former site for debarkation at Fell's Point, immigrants would arrive instead at Locust Point, formerly called Whetstone Point northwest of Fort McKinley. Serviced by the B&O, the facilities at Locust Point in South Baltimore near Federal Hill welcomed over one million persons who arrived during the period between 1868 to 1914 to make Baltimore one of the major "gateway" port cities, third only to New York and Boston. Of these, 80% entered from Bremen.

Starting in the 1790s, Bremen and then Bremerhaven was an important port on the North Sea near the Weser River west of Hamburg. Baltimore exported there tobacco and tropical products such as coffee and sugar and received linens, glassware and cutlery. After the 1830s, immigrants became an important part of the reverse flow. Having less trade with Britain or Ireland, most of the immigrants reaching, and staying in Baltimore, were German, giving Baltimore a German cast.

After the 1880s and the formation of the German Empire, the traditional Baltimore-Bremen connection via the North German Lloyd Line was maintained but now brought fewer immigrants from Germany but rather from farther east in Poland and Russia. Following 1868, most of the passengers from the steamships were immediately ushered onto the trains of the B&O lying alongside to go to the west. However, about 10% remained in Baltimore brought then by ferry to Fells Point from Locust Point.

In addition to the Germans, there were the Jews from Russia and Polish portions of the Austro-Hungarian Empire as well as Italians, Bohemians, Lithuanians, Poles and Greeks, reaching as much as 10% of the population. Blacks migrated from the tobacco fields to the city, reaching 20% of the total population from 1870 to 1900, far greater than other "gateway" port cities where European immigrants predominated far more.

The physical development of the city during this era was increasingly based upon urban mass transit, mainly to be used by the more affluent. Omnibuses of the 1840s first ran between the railroad stations and the hotels; those following regular street routes were replaced by the horse drawn trams in the 1860s; and then the electrified cog railways and trolleys of the 1890s that brought the white and the native-born to and from the suburbs. Multiple transit lines appeared, not necessarily well coordinated, with franchises offered by both the city and county governments. They were consolidated in 1900 into the "United Railways and Electric" with its large power plant on the Inner Harbor. The transit system was reorganized as the "Baltimore Transit Company" (BTC) in the 1930s on its way to abandoning the trolleys to the use of diesel powered busses.

There was increased separation of workplace and home, the physical separation of economic classes. Only 26% of the row houses were owner occupied; the others were rented but newly built multifamily tenement houses were very rare. Older larger houses were divided into smaller units rented to immigrants. Ethnic whites clustered around work sites in their two-story low cost row houses in neighborhoods that also included churches and municipal services such as branch libraries. Savings & Loan Associations in these ethnic enclaves as well as paternalistic employers such as those in Canton enabled home ownership that helped to ensure stability even in periods of depression.

Blacks mainly lived in the alley dwellings, and due to inadequate sanitation, also frequently died in these one hundred miles of alley housing owned by absentee proprietors. Although viewed mainly by outsiders in terms of social disorganization and disease, nevertheless many alley dwellers managed to develop adaptations to maintain order and continuity in their communities. There was actually little serious crime apart from the numerous victimless offenses such as bootlegging, numbers and speakeasies. The extended family structure that was characteristic of many alleys helped to achieve survival although dwellers were hired for only the most physically arduous tasks, paid the least, with the least job security and subject to the pervasive racism.

Between 1870 and 1900, the number of industrial establishments and the industrial immigrant labor force tripled. By the end of the century, larger scale conglomerates began to predominate. The large number of breweries coalesced into the single "Maryland Brewing Company"; the "American Can Company" united the canneries. Situated in Canton, the American Can Company employed many of the immigrant women living in East Baltimore. Financing these larger companies became national rather than local with headquarters moving to New York. What had been a town whose industries had been locally controlled now became a town of branches of national corporations. Most serious was the end of the independence of the B&O Railroad, now incorporated for a time into the system of its archrival Pennsylvania Railroad.

Industrial development shifted from the textile mills of Jones Falls at Hampden and Woodberry to include Highland Town, to South Baltimore, Locust Point and Curtis Bay. Still remaining were the textile mills producing cotton duck in Hampden twinned with Woodbery on either side along Jones Falls. A semi-isolated community arose with Druid Hill Park to the west, Wyman Park to the south and Roland Park to the north. Made up mainly of native-born Americans who had migrated from the South, Hampden-Woodberry became a stronghold of the KKK in the 1920s. Suspicious of outsiders, it remains relatively intact as the long closed mills that gave it sustenance are now being gentrified into restaurants.

In the highly important clothing industry, as machine production increased, artisans were displaced by unskilled labor; men replaced by lower wage women and children with even lower wage sweatshops with "take-out" work also proliferating. Eventually, clothing factories became the sites for thousands of workers with large capitalists, mainly German Jews, employing the masses of East European Jews. The department store similarly appeared. Hutzler Brothers was the largest. Moses Hutzler had emigrated from Bavaria in 1836 and helped found the *Har Sinai* Reform Congregation in 1847. Founded in 1858 with credit guaranteed by his father Moses, Abram Hutzler brought his two brothers into the firm in the next few years. Sited at Howard Street just north of Lexington Street, they created along with several others like Hochschild-Kohn, Stewarts and Bernheim's the fashionable west side retail district.

Hutzler's main "palace" store on Howard Street closed in the late 20th century. It stands abandoned in the center of a derelict block that had once been the center of Baltimore's retail downtown where the Baltimore Metro and the Light Rail still meet at a deteriorating Lexington Market that in the decade after 1900 once saw 50,000 shoppers each day.

The northeastern part of the city developed separately outside the city boundaries. No commuter railroad ran through it; the coastal plain was much easier to farm than the hilly western piedmont and remained far longer as farmland rather than suburban housing. The southeastern portion containing Canton and Highland Town also elected to remain outside the city boundaries in 1888 to protect against control of the poorly regulated slaughter houses and retention of Sunday opening of the beer houses.

In the southeast, a large working class German immigrant neighborhood of two-story two-three bay row houses arose adjacent to their workplaces such as metal works and shipyards. The neighborhood also contained German speaking churches, schools, and recreational organizations. However, it is important to remember that "Germany" did not exist as an entity until after 1871.

Those who are arrived as immigrants considered themselves as Bavarians, Prussians, Westphalians etc. Only after arrival and partial assimilation, was there membership in the ethno-cultural "German community."

Although most German organizations were based on religious as well as ethnic lines, the more secular Turnverein organization in 1850 in Baltimore was the nation's largest. Physical training, ideological education and sociability were its three cornerstones that brought them to unite also in favor of abolition of slavery and respond early to the call to arms by Lincoln after Fort Sumter. Another significant less ideological organization was the German *Schuetzen* recreational organization that leased the land in southwest Baltimore that is now Carroll Park.

The German influence had been strong from the beginnings of the town. In 1740, German-speaking immigrants from Pennsylvania had built the first brewery. Soon after, the first Reformed Church was built on Charles Street just north of St Paul's, to be succeeded by the still extant Otterbein Church built in 1785 on Conway near Sharp Street; the Lutherans built their Zion Lutheran Church on Gay Street, long the site of German-speaking services. Although their number was small, tensions still existed between those who wished an English-language service versus those who considered the German language and their faith intrinsically intertwined.

The surge of immigration in the 1840s renewed the growth of the German-speaking community to become the largest in the city, approaching 25% of the population. This German secondary wave of immigration tended to come to a greater degree from mainly Roman Catholic Bavaria. Their problem of assimilation was compounded by existing from the beginning within what was essentially an Irish Roman Catholic Church. Their claim of ethnicity was in conflict with the universality the Church sought to claim.

The first German-speaking Catholic Church of St Alphonsus in the 1840s was funded in part by King Ludwig I of Bavaria. The German-speaking Redemptorist Fathers (whose founder was St Alphonsus de Ligouri) were particularly active in the staffing German-speaking parish schools and encouraging the development of self-help savings & loan associations. Founded in Italy in the 1730s, the Redemptorist Fathers first arrived in America in Pittsburgh in 1839 to help found a German Catholic congregation in that city; then came to Baltimore in 1840. The site of the original St John the Evangelist German Catholic Church became St Alphonsus; another previously Irish St James Church became another German-speaking church in East Baltimore. Still others arose.

Each of the Catholic parishes, like the German Protestant Reformed and Lutheran Churches before them, developed schools that used German in their instruction. The most outstanding was Pastor Heinrich Sheib's school that arose at the Zion Lutheran Church, the city's oldest. In the 1830s, he started it anew on a non-sectarian basis with instruction in English as well as German. Non-sectarian and with a liberal rationalist orientation although associated with the Zion Church, it attracted children from the entire Baltimore community. "F. Knapp's German and American Institute" was another widely respected and even more fashionable school based on the enlightened principles of Johann Pestalozzi. Attended by such as H.L. Mencken, it too contained students from all portions of the Baltimore community and from elsewhere. The growth of these schools reflected the significance placed on education by the increasingly affluent German-speaking immigrants of the 1840s.

The German Jews numbered about 10,000, mainly from Bavaria where they were especially oppressed by restrictions on residence. Such German Jewish immigration ceased after opportunities improved under the rule of Bismarck in a now unified Germany after 1871. Particularly those affiliated with *Har Sinai* and *Oheb Shalom* who considered themselves Reform, saw their origins as German to a greater degree and adhered to the German language in their religious services into the next generation. It was considered a great innovation when Rabbi Benjamin Szold of *Oheb Shalom* agreed to give his sermon in English every other week as a concession to the younger English-speaking congregants. Maintaining the use of the German language in their social circles also served to separate themselves from the next wave of Jewish immigration for which the less highly developed Yiddish was their native tongue.

Like the rest of this German immigration of the 1840s, the Jews were an urban business group who joined into the clubs so characteristic of the German community. For example the German Liederkranz starting in 1836 was one of several singing clubs; the Germania Club starting in 1840 was the site for the upper business class by the 1880s; the Concordia Society starting in 1847 for the less affluent and more artistic. Jews belonged to these social organizations during the first German-speaking generation. For example, the Concordia Society sponsored an opera house in 1865 at Eutaw and German (later Redmond) Streets that was used by groups from both communities. Increasingly Jewish in membership, the Concordia Society disbanded after the opera house burned in 1891. Later, specifically Jewish social clubs arose such as the Phoenix and Clover Clubs. The separation into separate social circles following the 1870s has been attributed to the growing German Jewish assimilation that differentiated them from the ongoing successive non-Jewish German immigrants that joined the German-speaking clubs.

Until 1920, Germans in all their variety remained the largest single immigrant group while also tending to cluster in their own communities in many areas of West Baltimore. In face of the anti-German agitation during World War I, their separate identity diminished with the demise of the long lasting German-language daily *Deutsche Correspondent* in 1918 a highly important indicator.

In 1888, an additional 23 miles square miles of the county became the northern and western extensions of the city. This annexation included areas such as the duck cotton mills of Hampden-Woodbery along Jones Falls. Approved only narrowly along class lines, it was opposed by the workers organized under the Knights of Labor but supported by the mill owners as providing street paving and other services including tax breaks. Its post-World War II tawdriness remains documented by the Baltimore film maker John Waters in *Pecker*, a story of a young naïve local photographer.

Once more with the annexation of 1888, the opportunity for platting to include topographic features of the annexed area was avoided. Rather the decision was in favor of lower cost and shorter sighted platting of a grid designed for speculative building lots similar to the Poppleton Plan of the 1820s. However, digesting the annexation of this higher land of the piedmont later required modification of the earlier conventional grid Starting in 1902, developers were required for the first time to avoid plats that were "isolated, having no interconnections," and by 1908 required recognition of grades leading to more highly contoured streets.

Although not actually annexed until 1918, the suburb of Roland Park epitomizes the development of the northern suburbs that were serviced by the electrified trolleys of the late 19th century. The name derives from an early owner Roland Thornberry and the local Lake Roland. In 1857, Charles Street was extended north to reach the area of the Bellona Gunpowder Factory whose millrace was at the Junction of Roland Run and Jones Falls. Named after the Roman goddess of war, the mill was competitive with the Eleutherian Mills of E.I. DuPont on the Brandywine River. For example, the Bellona Mill provided the powder used at Fort McHenry in the Battle of Baltimore in 1814. It remained active despite several deadly explosions until its property was largely inundated by the formation of Lake Roland. The additions needed to the municipal water supply of Baltimore led to the impoundment of the waters of Roland Run by the Lake Roland Dam 225 feet above tidewater. A conduit then carried the water from Lake Roland to the Hampden Reservoir; then another conduit to the Mount Royal Reservoir. The system was complete by the 1870s with the connection to the Druid Lake Reservoir.

The area known as "Gravelly Hill" includes several neighborhoods of north Baltimore encompassed within the "Guilford-Homeland-Roland Park District" all developed by the Roland Park Company. Originally funded for long term development by a wealthy British investor's syndicate, it was able to maintain control over the development of a large segment of suburban Baltimore for over a half century. The area below 41st Street was included in the 1888 annexation, the area above in 1918.

Throughout this "District," there were the many roomed detached houses on large lots styled as Queen Anne, Shingle or Tudor. There still remains the cluster of private day schools so consistent with Baltimore's long standing history of private schooling for the children of the planter-based elite such as the Gilman School for Boys, the Bryn Mawr School for Girls and the Roland Park Country School as well as the Baltimore Country Club. Closely adjacent is the Friends' School. The advertisements proudly stated "one thousand restricted acres." Their restrictive covenants primarily included issues as to appearance and maintenance of non-commercial development but also prevented sales to blacks while an unwritten but rigid policy excluded Jews. Baltimore was noted for its exclusionary residential enclaves. Each ethnic and racial community was self-contained and self-absorbed; persons rarely crossed these boundaries to the detriment of a unified city.

Portions of the Roland Park District were on the former site of "Oakdale," the home of daughter of Charles Carroll of Carrollton at Falls Road and Cold Spring Lane that contained a house designed by Benjamin Henry Latrobe, the architect of the Roman Catholic Basilica. The estate was to the northwest of "Homewood," complete with ornamental lakes, originally built by her brother Charles Carroll Jr on land originally "Merryman's Lott." Guilford, the country estate of the Abell family that owned the *Baltimore Sun* was named after the Battle of Guilford Courthouse during the Revolutionary War where an even earlier owner of that estate had himself fought. Guilford was Baltimore's most fashionable suburb with its Sherwood Gardens. Its eastern border of York Road was the important dividing line of fashion.

Roland Park set the dominant tone of North Baltimore. The adjacent smaller suburb of "Wyndhurst" is spoken of as in the "vicinity of Roland Park" by those buying and selling its real estate to gain the cachet of its more fashionable neighbor. Its history is similar to the other northern suburbs that were uphill, upwind and upriver of the less desirable areas closer to the harbor. It also partook of the private school nature of the area in that much of the land was devoted to the Friends' School.

It is illustrative that it is bisected by Stony Run; its narrow residential streets can be entered from Roland Avenue on the west and Wyndhurst Avenue on the south rather than from the more heavily travelled Charles Street on the east. The southwest portion, called "Tuxedo Park," was an early portion developed by the same

Kansas City Land Company that developed Roland Park replicating the name of the famous exclusive suburb near New York City. The street names such as "Gladstone" also reflect its English pretensions. The later development of the larger tract adjacent to Roland Park followed a similar pattern but, unlike its larger neighbor, with lesser attention to protective covenants of all sorts.

Roland Park Country School has been since 1978 along Roland Avenue on the former estate of Charles Jerome Bonaparte, the grandson of Betsy Patterson and Jerome Bonaparte. Their brief marriage was annulled in order to enable the original Jerome Bonaparte to enter into a more politically advantageous marriage arranged by his brother Napoleon on the way to making him King of Westphalia. This was not before leaving behind a son called Jerome Napoleon Bonaparte who grew up in Baltimore living with his mother. A prominent member of Baltimore society, he was for example president of the exclusive Maryland Club in the 1850s at the time of its incorporation. Roland Park Country School was originally founded under the auspices of the Roland Park Company by the Howard sisters in 1894 in a house on Keswick Road. After some years on University Parkway, it now sits on its steeply hilly plot on Roland Avenue opposite the Gilman School for Boys and adjacent to St Mary's Seminary.

Plat One of Roland Park was the first laid out in 1891 north of Cold Spring Lane east of Roland Avenue on relatively flat land. It was closest to the tracks of the originally narrow gauge rickety Maryland & Pennsylvania (Ma & Pa) Railroad. Mainly carrying passengers from Towson into the city, the morning train, known as "The Milky Way," carried milk from the local farmers. Working under the direction of the Kansas City firm developing Roland Park, George Kessler designed Plat One just as he had designed residential developments in Kansas City where he had also been responsive to the contours of the land.

Plat Two of the new Roland Park suburb on more hilly land west of Roland Avenue was designed starting in 1901 by the Olmsted Brothers' firm situated in Brookline adjacent to Boston. The firm was successor to that founded by Frederick Law Olmsted Sr, the architect of Central Park and many others. The firm was noted for laying out streets to conform to the existing terrain to reduce erosion and building costs as well as create a picturesque appearance. The sylvan environment was what was called, after the British model, a "garden suburb." For the homeowners, the separation was now complete from their place of work, whether the bank or the warehouse. In order to preserve the residential nature of the area, businesses such as smelly stables were restricted; the first instance of land use planning that has since become universal. The first shopping mall was still-extant pseudo-Tudor fronted one containing but six stores that arose on Roland Avenue. The Roland Park Electric Railway ran on Roland Avenue directly from Baltimore City Hall twenty-four hours a day.

4.2. James Cardinal Gibbons and the American Catholic Church

James Cardinal Gibbons was born in 1834 to Irish parents then living on Gay Street in Old Town Baltimore. After onset of his father's illness from tuberculosis, the family returned to Ireland. In 1847, after his father's death, they returned to the United States to live in New Orleans. Gibbons trained at St Charles' College before graduating from St Mary's Seminary in Baltimore; and was ordained in June 1861. During the Civil War, Father Gibbons served as chaplain at Fort McHenry as well as pastor of a church at Locust Point.

In 1868, he started his rapid rise in the Catholic hierarchy. At age thirty-four, he was one of the youngest bishops in the Church. Apostolic Vicar in charge of North Carolina's seven hundred Catholics, he travelled the state. Bishop of Richmond in 1872, he became archbishop of Baltimore in 1877 and Cardinal in 1888, the second American to be designated.

Fig. 31 - Cardinal Gibbons

The Maryland Catholic Church had been first established by the Calvert's and carried on by Archbishop John Carroll. The original easy familiarity between upper class Catholics and Protestants was now modified by the growth of the "immigrant" Catholic Church. The latter was defined by ethnic enclaves that established an entirely Roman Catholic separatist culture.

In 1835, a number of prominent ministers had formed "The Protestant Association" to oppose "popery." In 1839, the escape from a convent of a nun in Baltimore led to rioting that threatened to burn the convent. An entire literature of "escaped nun" stories arose with titles such Priests' *Prisons for Women* that reinforced the distrust of this "foreign" religion.

The first of the clearly Irish churches was St Vincent de Paul parish in Old Town for those displaced by the German-speaking St John the Evangelist that had appeared in Old Town. The "Redemptorist" Order of the Most Holy Redeemer founded in 1732 was invited to provide German speaking priests starting at St Alphonsus in the 1840s with their seminary established in 1851 in Cumberland Maryland. With the immigrant, non-English-speaking church eventually after the 1880s came also the supporting parochial school in each parish and the lay societies for the support of the parish. The full panoply of support came into existence to establish the ethnic enclave as an urban ghetto in a mosaic of such.

Although committed to the formation of an American Catholic Church, Gibbons perforce permitted the development of national parishes that reflected the varied ethnic origins of the additional Catholics entering from eastern and southern Europe. Beyond the Germans, other churches represented the Italians, Poles. Bohemian, and Lithuanians as well as his own native Irish. The Poles, separated in Europe by the partition of their homeland lasting into 20th century, strove for ethnic unity and Polish nationalism in Baltimore. St Leo, named in honor of the new Pope Leo XIII, became identified as the Italian church in little Italy; St Wenceslaus for the Bohemians.

St Francis Xavier staffed since 1871 by the Josephites (Mill Hill Fathers) was established for blacks. St Joseph's Seminary was founded in Baltimore in 1888 to provide priests for the black parishes. Worship first started in 1863 in the chapel of the Oblate Sisters of Divine Providence, the first order of black Sisters founded by refugees from Haiti in the 1830s. The Franciscan Sisters of Mill Hill, invited by Cardinal Gibbons, arrived in Baltimore in 1881 to found an orphanage for black children. A separate black Catholic church arose; any message of ecumenism and Americanism was limited by the need for immigrants to seek security amongst their fellow compatriots.

The year Gibbons entered the archbishopric was also the year of the bitter B&O strike that involved many of his parishioners. To counteract the reduction in wages coincident with mechanization of factories, the Knights of Labor formed their first local assembly in Baltimore in 1878. At its height in 1886, sixteen local assemblies claimed twenty-five thousand members. Seventeen thousand mainly Catholic workers marched in that year's May Day parade. As many as 700,000 belonged nationwide for a short time before disintegrating after a series of unsuccessful strikes. Originally set up as a fraternal organization with secret rituals reminiscent of Freemasonry, it became more clearly a labor union seeking shorter working hours and the abolition of child labor. The American Federation of Labor also arose. Based more upon skilled labor organized in craft unions, they were less likely to be superseded by strike breakers from the large ranks of unemployed and new immigrants right off the boats at Locust Point.

By personal intervention with both Terence Powderly, the Catholic head of the Knights of Labor, and with the American Catholic hierarchy, Gibbons managed to avoid papal censure by the extremely conservative Pope Pius IX of those entering the Knights of Labor. In 1891, the *Encyclical De Rerum Novarum* by Leo XIII appeared to support Catholic membership in labor unions while also enjoining against class warfare and strike violence. However, an 1898 Papal letter seemed to reprimand such "liberalism." Addressed to Cardinal Gibbons, Pope Leo XIII attacked the tenets of "Americanism" as heretical. It reasserted the basic tenet of "Infallibility of the Pope" established at the First Vatican Council in 1869 to be absolute obedience to the papacy. The concern for individual behavior and social programs was deemed secondary to a primary commitment to religious observance. Particularly opposed by the pope was the apparent acceptance by the American hierarchy of the American doctrine of the separation of Church and State that Gibbons expressed to be in the spirit of John Carroll, the first archbishop.

Also one of the founders of the Catholic University of America in Washington DC; in the absence of a Papal Mission to the United States, Gibbons was the public face of American Catholicism in the national capital. He had close access to American presidents. For example, the golden jubilee of his ordination in 1911 was recognized by President Taft confirming his stance and that of American Catholicism as fully compatible with Americanism. His golden jubilee was also recognized by a parade of white-clothed young girls down the streets of Baltimore.

Even with a population of 500,000, it was only after 1906 that the first treated sewage system was started by the City of Baltimore to empty into the Back River Treatment Plant. Referenda had previously been turned down by voters on several occasions. The disinterest in adequate public infrastructure by the parochial political interests had prevailed until then unlike other major cities such as New York, Boston and Philadelphia. New York, for example had completed its iconic Croton reservoir in Westchester County by 1842; Boston had completed its first municipal water system in 1848 whereas Philadelphia had done so as early as 1815. The sudden concern with an adequate sewer system arose after the rebuilding after the Great Fire of 1904. There was need finally to accommodate the wastes engendered by large industrial companies considering moving to Baltimore in competition with other cities with more adequate municipal services.

With the rise in land values, the wasteful allocation of land to cesspools could no longer be justified on economic grounds even if health and aesthetic grounds did not suffice. Also for the first time, with the weakening in 1898 of "machine politics," the city could consider a comprehensive system rather than the piecemeal approach reflecting the political fiefdoms in each ward whose aldermen had acted in their own parochial interests. The wealthy, living on the higher also more abundant land, were less affected by the cesspool problem. They were loath to tax themselves for the benefit of the poor. However, Baltimore would finally no longer be known as the city "where sewage runs in the streets in front of the houses."

Similarly, the hitherto unfiltered water supply led to an epidemic of typhoid fever every summer, the highest rate in any American city. Along with sewage, the problem of providing an adequate safe water supply had been an issue throughout the 19th century. By 1800, the original sources in natural springs had dried up; wells had become contaminated. However, the impetus had been the inadequate pressure available to fight fires rather than any health concerns. Therefore, the first response was to erect pumps on the city streets to enhance the water supply available for firefighting.

The Baltimore Water Company was formed in 1804 to divert water from Jones Falls to a reservoir at the corner of Calvert and Centre Streets, also the site of the company's offices. In 1857, in conjunction with the purchase of the Baltimore Water Company by the City of Baltimore, water rights were purchased on Jones Falls north of Woodberry and Swann Lake (now Roland Lake) to create a 40 million gallon reservoir at Hampden, completed in 1861. Polluted by sediment by 1915, it was closed off and eventually became the site of Roosevelt Park adjacent to the Jones Falls Expressway.

In 1863, the plans for the Druid Hill Park would also include Druid Lake as a reservoir containing eventually 429 million gallons draining from Jones Falls and connecting with the Hampden and Mt Royal Reservoirs. In 1872, the inadequacy of the Jones Fall as a source of water became clear. Finally, in the 1880s, the Loch Raven Reservoir was built in Baltimore County to impound water from the Gunpowder River to be connected with a new reservoir at Lake Montebello and storage also at Lake Clifton. Nevertheless, a water famine occurred in 1910 when a drought coincided with the large increase in population.

Typhoid fever was eradicated by the chlorination of the water supply finally instituted in 1915 at the Montebello Plant. Additional filtration plants in the northwest at Lake Ashburton and the Liberty Dam and Reservoir dealt with the increased needs following the 1918 annexation. In 1924, a Metropolitan Water District was formed, connecting Baltimore County to the City of Baltimore water system, enabling post-World War II development in the County. In 1966, a water pumping station at Deer Creek began to draw water from the farther-off Susquehanna River.

The governmental and commercial district lay to the north of the original shoreline of Lombard Street, while the warehouses of the port were on filled in land below. To the west were the shops of the B&O Railroad. To the east were the industries of Canton and beyond. To the south of the Inner Harbor were the industries surrounding the old houses of Federal Hill. In the valley of Jones Falls were the mills and the houses of those who worked in them such as Hampden.

The Great Fire of February 1904 destroyed almost all the area of the former Baltimore Town, now downtown Baltimore. The more variegated usage and still remaining buildings from the early 19th century were replaced by widened streets and far higher buildings devoted to banking and other service industries. For example, Light Street was tripled in width; Pratt Street doubled. The widespread cobblestones and rough pavement were covered with asphalt. The retail district arose along Howard Street to the west and north of the old business district, while the alley dwellings surrounding the central business area persisted and increased as areas of disease to be avoided. Infant mortality as a measure of social disorder was persistently double that of white areas as was the crime rate, mainly black on black. Infectious disease such as typhoid and tuberculosis was commonplace.

Segregation became enshrined as government policy. As emigration of blacks increased following 1900, Baltimore was one of the first stops out of the South. Even as black population increased, available housing did not increase proportionately. The previous poor black neighborhood in southeastern Baltimore did expand to include for the more affluent a more attractive area in near northwest Baltimore along Druid Park Avenue. The purchase of a house across what had been a boundary line on the eastern side of McCulloh Avenue by a black professional family precipitated a bill in 1910 before the City Council. It established boundaries that designated all-white and all-black residential blocks. Once established in Baltimore, this confirmation of what had been unofficial segregation spread to cities throughout the South and the Border States.

At this same time, there were recurrent efforts to disenfranchise the black voters in Maryland. The failure of those efforts in Maryland differed from the more southerly states where poll taxes, literacy regulations and other constitutional "grandfather" clauses were instituted. The political sophistication and the tenacity of black participation in the electoral process in Baltimore reflected the uniquely large percentage of those who had been freed even before the Civil War. Baltimore had the largest free black population of any city in the country. Spared the effects of defeat and Reconstruction, the degree of white bitterness was also somewhat less in Maryland. Although the blacks were heavily burdened, a degree of independent economic opportunity and social organization provided a structure that would blossom later in the civil rights movement that found many of its leaders in the Baltimore black community.

A 1903 park plan was offered for the first time by the Olmsted brothers' firm outlining a system of parkways to unite the green spaces along the watercourses that define the topography of Baltimore. Although not carried out because of the problems caused by the 1904 Great Fire to the extent then possible, portions did already exist in the winding carriageways of Druid Hill Park and Clifton Park and streetcar connections between Druid Hill and Patterson Parks. Gwynns Falls and Stony Run were crossed by high bridges at only a few strategic points that preserved the underlying natural appearance. Part of the original Olmsted plan was realized by the formation of Leakin Park along the Gwynns Falls and Dead Run stream valleys in 1908. The park includes the country estate of Thomas Winans, whose wealth derived from the design of the flange wheels used on the early B&O locomotives.

1912 also saw the Jones Falls enclosed in an underground conduit with its superimposed Falls Way along with the Northern Central Railroad to carry coal from the Pennsylvania anthracite field traffic down the middle of the city. Bituminous coal carried by the Western Maryland Railroad from the Cumberland coal fields was also one of the main exports and provided fuel also for the steel industry centered on Sparrows Point. The Pennsylvania Steel Company plant there founded by the Pennsylvania Railroad became a part of Bethlehem Steel and the major employer of those living in East Baltimore.

The almost solidly Jewish clothing factories that took the place of the sweatshops were third only to those of New York City and Philadelphia. A bitter 1904 strike led to the recognition of the right of clothing workers to be union members with the formation of a local of the AFof L affiliated ILGWU (International Ladies Garment Workers Union). In 1913, the Amalgamated Clothing Workers succeeded in forming an arbitration system within Baltimore's largely men's clothing industry that gave representation to workers on grievance committees. Wages remained low until they rose with fuller employment during World War I, only to fall during the 1920s and the subsequent Depression.

By the 1830s, Baltimore had just edged out Philadelphia to become for a time the second largest city in the country, behind only the much larger New York. The *Baltimore Sun* started in 1837 by Arunah Shepherson Abell as a penny daily at a time when the city's six other dailies charged six cents; therefore designed to provide news to the masses. Born in 1806 of Puritan forbearers in East Providence Rhode Island, he apprenticed as a printer and gravitated to Philadelphia where he established The Public Ledger before coming to Baltimore. He and his partners established the *Baltimore Sun*, patterned after the New York paper of the same name to serve the literate mechanics and artisans, to provide them news of events rather than discussions of ideas.

Within a few years, it outsold all the other papers combined and remained the pre-eminent newspaper in Baltimore. Its success was assured by a commitment to speedy news including use of carrier pigeons and the then new telegraph. Its first coup in 1837 in printing within hours President Van Buren's message to Congress used the express trains of the Washington Branch of the B&O Railroad. It used a private pony express service to report on the Mexican War, which Abell also avidly supported. The newspaper was in the spirit of the booming city. Its first building expressly for its own purpose in 1851 was of cast iron, the first of that kind; in 1882, it was the first office building in Maryland to be illuminated by electricity. Its masthead for many years incorporated the train and the ship as the twin pillars on which the prosperity of Baltimore and its newspaper rested.

Fig. 32 - the Baltimore Sun Masthead

Treading carefully, despite Abell's secessionist sympathies, the newspaper managed to publish uninterruptedly during the Civil War while the city was under martial law and many other papers were suppressed. It managed to ignore most political and even many military happenings. During the war, the city lost its stride as did the newspaper. Deeply divided, the town was poisoned by animosities caused by the war. The southern market in which Baltimore had been dominant took many years to recover. Speaking for the "Democratic-Conservative Party," *The Sun* successfully opposed the continued disenfranchisement of Confederate sympathizers during the period immediately after the Civil War and helped reinstate the disenfranchisement of the black population.

With the removal of federal troops in February 1866, Maryland became a battleground as to the direction of Reconstruction. For the first time, there was the formation of a Unionist Republican Party in the state but, after the removal of the previous limitations on voter registration, the Democratic-Conservatives won the 1866 election. Despite the 1864 Maryland Constitution that had abolished slavery and instituted a loyalty test oath, the state was one the first of the former slave states to re-establish Democratic Party control by abolishing the test oath that excluded former Confederates. As a result, Maryland failed until modern times to ratify the 14th Amendment in 1868 assuring equality of accommodation as well as black suffrage under the 15th Amendment in 1870.

This "soft" Reconstruction was confirmed by the passage of a new Constitution in 1867 by a convention totally controlled by the Democratic Party. Racial segregation was re-established in Maryland; black schools were deprived of general tax revenues. Maryland gave its electoral votes to the Democratic Party presidential candidate in 1868 and thenceforth for a generation. With the loss of black political power, segregation and "Jim Crow" legislation denied the "colored schools" their fair share for the next hundred years.

Despite the destruction of their building during the 1904 fire, *The Sun* characteristically prided itself at not missing an issue. After the fire, the newspaper's new headquarter Ionic columned building arose at the very center of Baltimore at the corner of Charles and Baltimore Streets (known as "Sun Square"). Sold in 1910 by the founding family, its new publisher founded the *Evening Sun*. The impact of the new direction was also felt immediately in the support for the nomination of the reformist Woodrow Wilson for the presidency.

The papers date their greatest years starting in 1919 with the appointment of Paul Patterson as publisher with a commitment to be a newspaper "of national distinction" and to expand its presence in the Washington DC market. The morning and evening papers had separate staffs with the evening paper filled more with features and local breaking news. During the ensuing years of the early 20th century, the *Baltimore Sun* continued to be the "paper of record" and to represent the interests of the segregationist Democratic Party and the conservative business elements, particularly those of the B&O Railroad. Throughout its later history with international as well as national bureaus, the newspaper remained anti-New Deal and geared itself to the professional classes in the city. At first averting interest in the corruption of local politics; aroused by its competitors, it eventually became the acerbic well-spoken voice of good government against the machine politicians that organized the immigrant voting blocs in the 20th century.

Still considered one of the 10 best newspapers in the country in 1964, it was dropped from the list by 1974. Despite the increased local population, by 1980 its readership declined, while profits remained high. There was a dearth of Pulitzer Prizes along with low wages and absent staff benefits. Several strikes, led by the Newspaper Guild local that merged with that of Washington, disrupted publication. Sold to the outside interests of the *Los Angeles Times*, and then the *Chicago Tribune*, it has laid off staff in conjunction with the decline in readership and advertising that has affected newspapers everywhere.

4.3. H.L. Mencken and the *Baltimore Sun*

During its heyday, the *Baltimore Sun* provided a congenial home for the long time career of H.L. Mencken that brought Baltimore and its newspaper unusual prominence in the world of American letters.

Fig. 33 - Henry L. Mencken

Born in Baltimore in 1880 the grandson of a German-born cigar manufacturer, he inherited his father's ancestral skepticism about corrupt politicians and academic quackery. The tobacco trade in which his father worked was a particular preserve of the German community. His relatively prosperous grandfather had migrated from Saxony in 1848 in pursuit of even greater business opportunity rather than political liberty. An expression of this first Americanized generation of upright German immigrants, Mencken could recall the years when Baltimore was "Mobtown," a hotbed of "Know-Nothingism" in the 1850s opposed to immigrants such as when his own grandfather was injured in an election time riot. He never forgot what an angry mob can do to a helpless person.

Mencken lived almost his entire life in the family home in an Italianate 3 story row house at 1524 Hollins Avenue bought new in what was then the highly acceptably middle class Union Square in West Baltimore. His family would spend their summers at what was then still semi-rural Mount Washington. Mencken describes his mother shopping at the open-air Hollins Market nearby. During his lifetime, that area of Southwest Baltimore degenerated into one of its worst slums filled with murders and drugs.

Looking back, he describes his in-town neighborhood of the 1880s: "The [modest] two-story houses that were put up [when I was young] all had a kind of unity....they were built of red brick, with white trim - the latter either of marble or of painted wood. The builders of the time were not given to useless ornamentation: their houses were plain in design and restful to the eye. A long row of

them were to be sure monotonous, but it escaped being trashy....".
Many such rows survive, but the trees are gone, and new store fronts,
plate glass front doors and concrete steps, and other such horrors
have pretty well corrupted their old placid beauty.

A voracious reader since childhood particularly of Mark Twain, he
attended the Baltimore Polytechnic, one of the city's elite public high
schools, despite its curriculum ostensibly contrary to his literary
interests. He continued all his life to use libraries; the Enoch Pratt
Circulating Library was his mainstay but the Peabody Library
provided a cubicle for him as a researcher that it retains dedicated to
his works. There is also a room dedicated to him and his literary
pursuits in the main building of the Enoch Pratt Free Library to
which he bequeathed his private library.

Without further formal education, he became a reporter in 1899
for the shoestring *Baltimore Herald*; and then in 1905 for the *Baltimore
Sun*. After 1910, he wrote mainly, but not exclusively, for the *Evening
Sun*. He loved Baltimore, and its access to what he called the great
protein factory of the Chesapeake Bay. He kept it the center of his
life as it deteriorated around him and as he became world famous. He
wrote his column until the late 1930s and then intermittently until
1948 when he experienced a stroke. He was primarily a
newspaperman who wrote his incisive satire about local politics. He
was undaunted by World War I anti-German propaganda when the
long standing name of German Street was patriotically changed to
Redwood in honor of a Marylander killed in the war. In an act of

defiance, he joined the Germania Club in 1916; but was also less appropriately oblivious of the consequences of Nazism in the 1930s.

Mencken became nationally known for his writings as a literary critic of *The Smart Set* starting in 1908, the *New Yorker* of its day; then as the scoffing social critic "debunking" editor of *The American Mercury* from 1924 to 1933. Coining the term "Bible Belt," he was a constant critic of its culture and customs. He was an integral member of the American literary scene in the destruction of the once "genteel literary tradition." This led to friendship with such luminaries as Theodore Dreiser, Sinclair Lewis, F. Scott Fitzgerald and James Branch Cabell. His own writing of successive editions of his magnum opus *The American Language*, the study of the divergence of British and American English, still assures him recognition.

An early proponent of Frederick Nietzsche, Mencken throughout his life supported the role of the extraordinary individual in opposition to the "booboisie" of the masses, the "Babbitt's" and the evangelist Billy Sundays. He saw all government as conspiracy against the exceptional man: its one permanent object is to oppress him and cripple him. This also led to his almost visceral hatred of President Franklin Roosevelt and the New Deal based on their "collectivism" and the subsequent eclipse of his *The American Mercury* after 1933 as well as his championing of Ayn Rand in later life.

The streets to the northwest south of North Avenue run in a tilt parallel and perpendicular to Reistertown Road. Similarly, the unusually wide Druid Park Avenue and McCulloh Streets follow the same pattern from North Avenue to Druid Hill Park. The widest of

Baltimore's streets, Eutaw Place between Dolphin Street and North Avenue (until 1888 the boundary of the city) was divided in the center by a narrow mall, complete with fountains with statuary and trees. Still particularly prominent at the crest of the hill at Lanvale Street is the gilded statue and fountain celebrating Francis Scott Key admiring the "Star Spangled Banner" from a rowboat below.

Fig. 34 - Francis Scott Key Monument

The houses bordering the park were first owned by those German Jews who dominated the city's retail and apparel industries in the 1870s with the stately domed *Oheb Shalom* and Byzantine-styled Madison Avenue synagogue of Baltimore Hebrew Congregation and the exclusive Phoenix Club at 1505 Eutaw Place. The ornate Marlborough Apartments still dominates the street. To the southeast was the non-Jewish portion below North Avenue of Mt Royal with its Episcopal Church and Confederate Monument on Mount Royal

Avenue commissioned in 1903 by the United Daughters of the Confederacy. This is to be contrasted at the Mount Royal Avenue entrance to Druid Hill Park to the much larger monument dedicated to the Union soldiers and sailors commissioned by the Maryland state legislature. Both Bolton and Mount Royal were names of former estates in the area; Whitelock the name of an estate owner. The home of the Alexander Brown family, Mondawin was derived from the Indian word for maize.

The change that occurred in the character of Eutaw Place was to be replicated successively in the real estate pattern of Baltimore. Segregation was a matter of public law in Baltimore from 1910. When struck down by the Maryland courts in 1918, restrictive covenants were substituted until struck down by the Supreme Court in 1948 only to be enforced sub-rosa to ensure de-facto segregation. There was a three-tier real estate market: Christian, Jewish and Black. Successively, areas formerly entirely closed to Jews became entirely Jewish as they were abandoned by non-Jews; then become open to blacks only to be abandoned by whites to become all black. Unique among major cities at that time, it had both large immigrant Jewish and black populations.

4.4. The Cone Sisters and the Baltimore Museum of Art

On the walls of their several apartments at the then luxurious Marlborough Apartments on Eutaw Place, Dr Claribel and Etta Cone placed their art. Starting in 1901 and particularly after 1905 and then in the 1920s, funded by their family textile mills in North Carolina,

175

the two spinster sisters amassed one of the largest collections of Matisse, Picasso and other modern masters.

Herman Kahn (Cone) born in Germany in 1828, immigrated to Richmond Virginia in 1846. After establishing a grocery in Jonesboro Tennessee in 1856, he married in Richmond Helen Guggenheimer of Natural Bridge Virginia. They had a total of thirteen children. Claribel, the fifth, was born in 1864 and Etta, the ninth, was born in 1870. Frederic, the youngest was born in 1878; none of these three married; they eventually set up joint households in Baltimore's Marlborough Apartments under Miss Etta's management.

Confederate sympathizers in Unionist East Tennessee, the family waited out the war on a farm. He then moved the family from Jonesboro to Baltimore in 1871 to set up a wholesale grocery business based mainly on their Southern connections. The Cone family also became part of the extensive German Jewish community centered on Eutaw Place including many of their own extended family. With the Marlborough built at # 1707 in 1905, the apartment building became a prestigious address for the German Jewish elite.

By the 1890s, the two eldest Cone sons had become owners of several Southern cotton mills with the Cone Manufacturing Company eventually centered in Greensboro North Carolina. The Cone Mills, including the largest denim manufacturing facility in the world, created a community surrounding the mills that provided unusually complete health and other benefits for their employees. The Moses Cone Memorial Hospital still exists although the mills are no longer family-owned.

Fig. 35 – Dr Claribel Cone

A picture when nineteen years old shows Claribel not as a pretty girl but a handsome one, straight of back and large with a challenging demeanor. Claribel was both the elder of the two sisters and the more dominant. Independent of conventional roles for women, she went to Baltimore's Western High School and then in 1886 to Baltimore Women's Medical College, the first such in the South founded in 1882. She then studied gynecology at Johns Hopkins before residency training at the Women's Medical College of Philadelphia and the Blockley Hospital in Philadelphia.

Returning to Baltimore in 1895, she started a career in research and teaching as Professor of Pathology at the Women's Medical College and Pathologist at the Good Samaritan Hospital. She also worked as a colleague of William Welch and William Osler at Johns

Hopkins. From 1903 to 1906, she studied under the then leading Karl Weigert at the Pathology Institute in Frankfurt-on-Main and later returned to Munich Germany alone to work during World War I between 1916-1921. Etta, upon graduation from Western High School in 1885, took on the role as family housekeeper for her elder sister, a subordinate position that continued until the death of Dr Claribel in 1929.

Gertrude (born 1872) and Leo (born 1874), Stein first entered the Cone family orbit in 1892 when they joined their own extended Bacharach family in Baltimore following the death of their parents in California. Etta went to concerts at the Peabody and viewed art at the Walters under the spell of Leo Stein, already interested in art and literature before going to Harvard. After her own graduation from Radcliffe in 1897, Gertrude Stein entered for a time the Johns Hopkins Medical School. Dr Claribel and Gertrude Stein travelled together daily on the trolley to the Johns Hopkins Hospital on Broadway from their home on Eutaw Place. They appeared as an example to more conventional young women such as Saidie Adler for their self-confidence and independence. The Steins occasionally attended the Saturday evening salon that Dr Claribel established, a forerunner of their own much more famous salon in Paris at 27 Rue de Fleurus and the one their elder brother Michael established around the corner at Rue Madame.

In 1898, brother Moses Cone first gave his sister Etta a small amount of money to buy art to brighten up their family home. Her purchase of several small, rather conventional for their time, paintings by Theodore Robinson was the start of the Cone Collection. Miss Etta followed this same pattern throughout the next fifty years as the collection wandered into much more radical artists, but not their most radical statements. From the start, she bought what she liked that would decorate her home. Starting in 1901, under the tutelage of Leo Stein, Etta began to travel in Europe visiting art galleries. However, her interest was in content compatible with her tastes rather than a more formal aesthetic dealing with the artist's use of the physical properties of the paint and canvas that interested Leo Stein.

With their father's death, each of the sisters acquired a small inheritance that provided the income for their early art purchases. After 1905 in Paris, Etta bought her first Picasso urged by Gertrude Stein as a "romantic charity" to help out the artist. The drawings came to form the core of her large Picasso collection. That same year following the Steins' much more controversial choice, Etta purchased her first drawings from Matisse, later the touchstone of their collection and close friend. At the time of her purchase, Matisse was so poor and discouraged so s to plan to burn his paintings to secure their insurance.

The collection grew much more after 1921 when both sisters began to travel in Europe every summer. With their allowance increased along with a favorable exchange rate, they began to amass a large number of works by Matisse. Claribel acquired the iconic *Blue Nude* from the Quinn Collection in 1926 along with works by Cézanne, Renoir and Gauguin.

After Dr Claribel's death in 1929, Matisse drew a noteworthy series of studies of both Claribel and Etta. In December 1930, Matisse caused a stir when he visited Etta's home in Baltimore, now widely recognized for the first time as one of the largest collections of his works in the United States. In their private apartment on no longer fashionable Eutaw Place, the Cone sisters had created a shrine to Matisse and his harem of women. Etta worshipped Matisse as an artist who committed to canvas the sensuous life she did not otherwise permit herself to experience. Etta Cone also carried on her "romantic charity" by buying works of the young artists at the Maryland Institute of Art and chose to leave her collection to the Baltimore Museum of Art to become one of its centerpieces.

The Baltimore Museum of Art (BMA) was founded in 1914 to provide an art museum for Baltimore as part of the plan to renew the city after the Great Fire of 1904. The Walters Art Museum was not yet fully open to the public. The story is told that the Baltimoreans were stung by the fact that a city as minor as Toledo Ohio already had an art museum open to the public whereas a city as significant as Baltimore had not. The group organized in 1911 by A.R.L. Dohme (of the chemical firm of Sharp & Dohme) was called the "Citywide Congress for the Founding of a Museum." Their early home was at the southwest corner of Mt Vernon Place, the house of Mary Elizabeth Garrett, the daughter of John W Garrett.

The Museum opened in 1929 in Wyman Park on land donated by Johns Hopkins University within a classical temple designed by John Russell Pope. The leading Beaux-Arts architect of the time, Pope was favored as the architect by Mary Frick Garrett Jacobs. The sculptured lions at the entrance are by Adolph Weinman, a sculptor favored by John Russell Pope for whom he designed the sphinxes at the Scottish Rite Temple in Washington DC and the pediment of the National Archives. Trained with Augustus Saint-Gaudens and Daniel Chester French, Weinman was particularly noted for his lions on the Pennsylvania Station in New York City.

Unlike the Walters Art Museum, there would be wider diversity of origin of collectors as well as their collections. One of those collections was that of Jacob Epstein. He was one of the second large wave of Jewish immigration that came to Baltimore starting in the 1880s. Unlike most other Jews who tended to live in East Baltimore, Epstein's family first settled in South Baltimore. Born in Lithuania in 1864 what was then part of the Russian Empire, and starting as a young peddler, he eventually owned a very successful mail order business called "The Baltimore Bargain House." It became successful by furnishing goods to the mainly Jewish peddlers and then retailers particularly throughout the smaller Southern towns. Around 1910, his company was the largest employer in Baltimore, second only to the B&O Railroad.

Always the largest single contributor to the Associated Jewish Charities that he founded as a means of uniting the German and East European segments of the Jewish community, he was also closely associated with the founding of the BMA. His extensive collection of old masters ranging from Raphael to Van Dyck, from Rembrandt to

Rodin and Titian is an important part of the museum, recognized at least in part by a designated gallery.

Sadie Adler May was the young girl who had noted the independence and confidence displayed by her distant relatives Dr Claribel Cone and Gertrude Stein. She and her sister Blanche were in turn the source of a large collection of contemporary art at the BMA illustrated by works such as by Miro and Tanguy. They ranged deliberately and non-competitively into abstract art and surrealism that had been avoided by the Cone Sisters and where the Cone Collection left off. Unlike so many collectors of the time, both the Adler sisters bought directly for museums, to be seen by others.

Born in Baltimore in 1879, Saidie Adler's father Charles Adler was a wealthy shoe manufacturer at a time when Baltimore was a center for the shoe trade. He had immigrated from Hesse-Cassell in the 1850s via Bremen to Baltimore after having settled for a time in Germantown Maryland. The youngest of six children, the tiny Saidie grew up in Bolton Hill, and, along with her sister Blanche, attended the progressive Sarah Randolph School for Girls on Eutaw Place.

She married within her class a cousin Albert Carl Lehman of Pittsburgh, head of the very large Blaw-Knox Steel Company, with whom she had a son who became mentally retarded after an illness. She was devoted to him while he lived apart from her in a residential school. Divorced after twenty years of marriage, she then remarried another recently widowed Pittsburgh industrialist Herbert May before finally once again divorcing after a short time. An amateur artist in oils, she enrolled in an atelier in Paris. After her second divorce, she then carried on an independent life during the interwar years with a younger male companion, a fellow artist who also became her protégé. Without a fixed address, she travelled from season to season, spending fall and spring with family in Baltimore.

Heavily influenced by Hans Hofmann, the teacher of post-World War II school of American abstract expressionists, she was considered particularly adventurous in her tastes. Unlike the more selective Museum of Modern Art in New York, her contributions were welcomed by the newly formed BMA. She helped Marc Chagall and Andre Masson and his family escape from Nazi-occupied Europe. She extensively collected Masson's work among others such as early Pollock and Motherwell who gained from their association with Masson during his stay in New York. Her sister Blanche Adler remaining unmarried and living in Baltimore, was an active collector of prints and drawings and selflessly bought to help create that department at the BMA.

4.5. The Frick Family and Baltimore's Golden Age

Fig. 36 - Mary Frick Garrett Jacobs

Born in 1851, Mary Frick was the grand dame of Baltimore with her in-town mansion, country estate called "Uplands" near Catonsville and a "cottage" in Newport designed by John Russell Pope. In 1872, she had married Robert Garrett II, the elder son of John Work Garrett and his father's short term successor as president of the B&O Railroad. Dead in 1896 at forty-three after a long period of illness, his widow remarried in 1902. After drawing up a pre-nuptial agreement to separate their fortunes, she married Henry

Barton Jacobs her husband's personal physician. She lived until 1936 aged eighty-five in her mansion on the south side of West Mount Vernon Place.

Dr Jacobs was born in Hingham Massachusetts, trained at Harvard College and Harvard Medical School before becoming Robert Garrett's personal physician. A distinguished expert in the treatment of tuberculosis, he was active in National Tuberculosis Association and an avid collector of Laennec memorabilia, the great French physician who had invented the stethoscope.

The original mansion at #11 bought by John W Garrett in 1872 as a wedding present to the young couple was redesigned in 1884 by Stanford White on the young Garrett's accession to the railroad presidency. Incorporating #9, it was covered in brownstone and had a large entrance portico inserted. It was in the then fashionable eclectic neo-Renaissance style including a Tiffany dome, the latter altered many times to meet the owners' exacting standards. They entertained lavishly. For example, at a dinner in 1892, ninety Maryland terrapins were used in the soup course and the New York Philharmonic performed.

The house was then altered by John Russell Pope in 1902 on Mary Frick Garrett's remarriage to incorporate #7 to be covered with Caen stone. The new portion included the library, art gallery and theater. The mansion thus sprawls over four lots incorporating the four townhouses at #7, 9, 11 and 13 West Mt Vernon Place. The art gallery containing her Old Master paintings by artists including Rembrandt, Hals and van Ruisdael was bequeathed to the BMA.

Now since the 1960s used by the Engineer's Club, the house has been restored in large part to reflect Baltimore's Golden Age of the late 19th and early 20th century

Stanford White was the flamboyant partner in the leading architectural firm of McKim, Mead and White when he designed the interior of the Garrett house in the 1880s. Born in 1853, he was a protégé of Henry Hobson Richardson. The latter trained at L'Ecole des Beaux-Arts in Paris and was the founder of the Richardsonian-Romanesque style in the United States. White is famous for the Washington Arch in Washington Square in New York City as well as the original Madison Square Garden where he was shot in 1906 by a jealous husband. White designed several churches in Baltimore in the 1880s along with the Garrett Mansion that expresses his adherence to the neo-Renaissance style of the brownstone era.

John Russell Pope was of the next generation of fashionable architects   trained at L'Ecole des Beaux-Arts in Paris. A protégé of Charles McKim, he also trained at the American Academy in Rome founded by McKim. Early in his career as an architect, Pope found work in altering mansions such as the Garrett-Jacobs Mansion in Baltimore and the McLean Mansion on I Street in McPherson Square in Washington DC to create room for grand entertaining.

The trajectory of the prosperous Frick family traces the development of the important German element in Baltimore in the 19th century. The original settler John Conrad Frick (1688-1761) emigrated in 1732 from the Rhenish Palatinate, as did so many other early immigrants to Philadelphia. He helped found Germantown near

Philadelphia where he lived until his death. In the second generation, his fourth son Peter (1743-1827) moved to Baltimore. Painted by Peale, he was a successful merchant and a member of the first City Council after the city was chartered in 1797. In the third generation, his second son William (1790-1855) was a leading maritime lawyer, judge and, in association with Roger Taney, a leader of the Jacksonian party in Maryland. He was appointed Collector of the Port of the District of Maryland by President Jackson in 1837. He helped create the Department of the Humanities at the University of Maryland. A younger brother born in 1793 was Dr George Frick who published the first treatise on eye diseases in America and was an instructor at the University of Maryland Medical School at Greene and Lombard Streets.

In the fourth generation, the eldest son William Frederick (Sloan) Frick (1817-1905) trained at Baltimore City College and Harvard College (1835) when he associated with Henry Wadsworth Longfellow and Charles Sumner while in Cambridge. Probably the founder of the family fortune in the 19th century, he was admitted to the bar and served on the governing boards of many of Baltimore's major companies including the B&O Railroad, Consolidated Coal and Consolidated Gas. Also concerned with public education, he was president of the Baltimore School Board.

In the fifth generation, his elder daughter (1851-1936) was the Mary Sloan Frick who married Robert Garrett and served as the doyenne of Baltimore social circles for many years. Her elder brother James Swan Frick (1848-1927) went to University of Virginia (1869) and the University of Maryland Law School. He joined his father's law practice before retiring early in 1890 to live the life of a clubman. Charlcote House, his home in Guilford, remains as designed in 1916-1917 in the grand neo-Georgian residential style of John Russell Pope's great era.

CHAPTER 5
THE POST-INDUSTRIAL CITY. 1945-1975

5.1. To Baltimore County

Baltimore remained a segregated city; Maryland remained a southern state both ruled by the Democratic Party. Maryland in the 1920s had the largest state memberships in the KKK. The Republican Party in Baltimore, to the extent it was permitted to exist, represented black voters but remained outside the power structure. Areas of black population were broken up into several assembly and congressional districts preventing representation. Coupled were restrictive registration requirements that further discouraged voting by blacks.

William Curran was the Democratic Party leader in the city during the 1930s until his death in 1946; Jack Pollack led the Jewish vote in the 4th District of northwest Baltimore from his Trenton Democratic Club in the 3700 block of Lower Park Heights Avenue, the only suburban area where Jews were permitted to live. The 4th District later became a bastion of the black voter.

Starting in the 1870s, the area east of Jones Falls from President Street east to Eden Street and from Pratt Street north to Eastern Avenue was the home of both East European Jewish and Italian immigrants. The original Orthodox Lloyd Street synagogue (Baltimore Hebrew Congregation) had been the center of the German Jewish community of the 1840s. Now more prosperous, that community moved to Northwest Baltimore. It was centered around the Baltimore Hebrew Congregation synagogue (now a 7th Day Adventist Church) on Madison Avenue below North Avenue. It was now no longer Orthodox but had become Reformed in its orientation to ritual and level of observance. The building of the "middle of the road" *Oheb Shalom* was also at Eutaw Place and Lanvale Avenue (now a Masonic Temple of the Prince Hall Masons); the Reform *Har Sinai* moved in 1894 nearby to Bolton and Wilson Streets. The Conservative *Chizuk Amuno* was also adjacent to Lake Drive and Druid Lake Park. The progressive Park University School near Druid Hill Park was established in 1912. It offered an alternative for Jewish boys excluded under a rigid quota system from most other boys' private schools.

The second wave of Jewish immigration from Poland and Russia took their place in the old area of East Baltimore around Lombard Street working in their "putting out" sweatshops. The older larger houses, formerly inhabited by Germans and Irish, now converted to tenements, offered low rents to accommodate the newer immigrants. The Jewish Educational Alliance, equipped with showers as well as classrooms and a gym, was situated from 1925 to 1951 on East Baltimore Street in Old Town. There also were the other smaller synagogues and the *Workmen's Circle Lyceum*. The "Russian Night School" founded by Henrietta Szold, daughter of the rabbi of *Oheb Shalom*, taught English to immigrants. The business center was on the 1000 block of Baltimore and Lombard Streets where the smell of corned beef still pervades the few remaining premises.

The Russian Jewish immigrant community followed west and north beyond Eutaw Place at various stages. In the 1930s and 40's, they settled along Liberty Heights Avenue to Forest Park with its detached houses with grassy plots of land as a way stop to upper Park

Heights Avenue starting in the 1960s to Pikesville and beyond. As the Jews and Germans moved away from the southern district of East Baltimore, the Italian community coalesced in this area with the remnant still now called "Little Italy."

The nucleus around which Little Italy first formed were stone masons from Genoa who came on the ships bringing marble from Italy and carrying grain back to Northern European ports. By 1879, Archbishop Gibbons agreed to form the Italian national parish of St Leo close to the President Street Station of the Philadelphia, Wilmington & Baltimore Railroad. Not the only center of Italian population, it was however, a low rent overcrowded area made up mainly of fruit peddlers and laborers on construction projects such as those after the 1904 fire. Property acquisition by immigrants started early along President Street and farther east with extended families living in adjacent houses. The first generation immigrant population reached its height of nearly 2000 by 1920 with men and women employed in the clothing factories forming an Italian-speaking local of the Amalgamated Clothing Workers. Restaurants opened in the mid-1930s arising from the Italian grocery stores. During World War II, the workers in the local shipyards had their meals there.

5.2. The D'Alesandro Family and Baltimore Politics

Although low rents and proximity to transportation brought Italians there, it was the presence of St Leo that kept them there. As a national parish, it had no territorial boundaries and Italians from elsewhere would return for baptisms and weddings. The Italian

Pallotine fathers were assigned to serve the church; a school and orphanage were built.

Born in 1903 to immigrant parents, one of the parochial school's graduates was Thomas D'Alesandro Jr. He headed the committee in 1929 to build a new school for St Leo's whose construction was also aided by the contributions of the several Italian building contractors.

After graduation from Calvert School of Business, he sold insurance thus bringing him in contact with the entire larger community. Trading on his community connections as its native son, D'Alesandro was elected to the Maryland House of Delegates at an early age in 1926, to the Baltimore City Council in 1935 and to the United States Congress as a New Deal Democrat from 1939 until 1947. He won his first city-wide election as mayor of Baltimore in 1947 to serve for three terms until 1959. His election, acclaimed by the inhabitants of little Italy, marked the political maturity of the first generation of this later immigration.

Fig. 37 - Thomas D'Alessandro Jr

His son, Tommy D'Alesandro III, groomed for politics since birth, emerged as a liberal Democrat of the Kennedy stripe. Elected by a large multiracial majority, he had the misfortune to be elected mayor in 1967 just prior to the riots and declined to run for re-election. The youngest daughter Nancy married and moved to California to become a member of the U.S. Congress from San Francisco and the first woman and Italian-American to become Speaker of the House.

Although the rate of white home ownership was one of the highest in the country, the rate of black home ownership was one of the lowest. With the automobile and the relatively poor quality of the public schools, whites moved even beyond the city limits, expanded for the last time in 1918 when it tripled in size to its now nearly one hundred square miles.

Development in the eastern reaches of Baltimore lagged behind that in the west. By 1900, streetcar service had extended in northeast Baltimore from the former city line of North Avenue as far as the community of Hamilton. Somewhat later service was extended to Belair Road farther east along the Herring Run watershed to areas like Gardenville and Overlea, which remained rural somewhat longer. The issue of urban amenities such as water, sewage and better roads versus increased taxes had prevented annexation; the large number of subdivisions that had already arisen in northeast Baltimore by 1918 finally ended the argument in favor of annexation to the city. An amendment to the state constitution in 1948 prevented any further annexation without the approval of the voters involved. The boundaries of the city of Baltimore were not to change.

The black percentage of the population of Baltimore City, always high, increased further with migration of the former tenant farmers during the Depression. The neighborhood of Druid Avenue and McCulloh was where the black lawyers and doctors lived. Upton was the name of the former estate in the area that was developed after the horse cars were introduced. Cab Calloway grew up in Upton. The Sharp Street M.E. H. built its granite church at Dolphin and Etting in 1896; Union Baptist moved from downtown to Druid Hill Avenue in 1905; Bethel A.M.E moved into the impressive neo-Gothic former St Peter's Episcopal Church on Druid Hill Avenue in 1911 with the only slightly less impressive Sharpe Street Methodist Episcopal Church nearby.

Unable to try clothes on downtown, Pennsylvania Avenue was the central business artery and the Royal Theater the showplace. In the 1300 block, the theater had its greatest success in the 1930s and 1940s as the local stop on the segregated theater circuit that included the Apollo in Harlem and the Howard on Washington's U Street. A different name band such as that of Duke Ellington and singers such as Ella Fitzgerald were billed each week. Pennsylvania Avenue was also one of the boundaries of what was called "The Lung Block" where tuberculosis was prevalent. Poverty plagued the black community as unemployment, always high in the 1920s, became even greater in the 1930s. Last hired, they were the first fired.

Despite the reluctance of traditional states-rights Governor Ritchie to accept federal funds, Mayor Howard Jackson did so somewhat more aggressively while still bridling against federal power in the name of its erosion of local government. One of the fruits was the new central building of the Enoch Pratt Free Library with its art deco atrium and the beginnings of slum clearance to be replaced by public housing. Slums with overcrowded dilapidated housing had long been considered to be breeding ground not only of poverty but of crime, disease and immorality. Creating decent housing was felt to be "uplifting," to break the cycle of poverty, to rehabilitate health and character and remove the blight on the city by slum clearance.

The Housing Authority of Baltimore City (HABC) was founded in 1937. Like such activities elsewhere, in the name of slum clearance, it built segregated projects that not merely re-enforced segregation. At times poor but integrated neighborhoods were destroyed in the name of slum clearance alone. Moreover, the extended family structure that had helped to maintain a degree of order in the street life of the "slums" was destroyed as evidenced by the eventual recent demolition of the Edgar Allan Poe Homes, one of the first built in 1939. With the New Deal and President Franklin Roosevelt, the black vote shifted from the impotent Republican Party to the Democratic Party. For example, former Republican black City Council member William Fitzgerald became a Democrat and had a role in administering federal WPA funds.

The greatest impact of the New Deal was the rise of unionism; the greatest impact of that rise was the development of the unionization of seamen and port workers centered in Fell's Point and the Port of Baltimore. Long the "true proletariat of the Western world," seamen were fed poorly and slept in cramped unhealthy quarters on unsafe ships. The "Anchorage" at the corner of Broadway and Thames Street (now the touristic Admiral Fell Inn) was from 1892 a "Christian" boarding house; after 1929 the Seaman's YMCA and then, taken over by the Waterfront Unemployed Council in 1934, a center for union activity during the strikes of the 1930s.

Known as the "Baltimore Soviet," the men took over the distribution of federal relief funds and created more favorable hiring practices under their own auspices apart from their previous ineffectual union. Attacked by the ship owners, a strike was called in 1936 under the leadership of Joe Curran to create fairer hiring practices in union halls, better pay and shorter working hours. The white but not the black Baltimore local of the dock workers' union recognized the strike picket lines, albeit only briefly. However, eventually, under the auspices of the NLRB, the multi-racial National Maritime Union (NMU) under Joe Curran was established and the goals of the 87 day strike were accomplished.

During World War II, the black population of Baltimore further increased by 20%, there was migration from the tenant farms of the Eastern Shore and from farther South. World War II brought jobs to Baltimore shipyards and aircraft plants, even temporarily to some blacks. Western Electric employment tripled, Westinghouse increased six-fold. Bethlehem-Fairfield Shipyards employment approached 50,000. In 1943 when the Liberty ship named after the black leader Frederick Douglass was launched, no notice was paid that he had been a worker as a slave at the predecessor of that shipyard. Moreover, in repetition of when he and other blacks had been driven out in the 1830s, and like the case of the black caulkers being attacked in the 1850s, the attempt to provide training during World War II for black riveters was opposed by whites who went out on strike.

Throughout this time, The *Baltimore Afro-American* was the community's voice from its office in the 600 block of N. Eutaw Street of the happenings scorned by mainstream newspapers. Carl Murphy was a graduate of Douglass High School, Howard University, and Harvard and, most remarkably, a student of philology at the University of Jena in Germany. Under him, the newspaper grew from a Baltimore weekly to a national chain. It had at mid-20th century a circulation of 200,000, the largest of any black newspaper in the country, published in eight regional editions including one in Washington DC.

Fig. 38 - Carl Murphy

Run by the Murphy family since 1892, it has since come into the possession of the Oliver family, a Murphy descendant. Jake Oliver was, now in the 21st century, the publisher committed to maintain a family tradition. Oliver recalled, when interviewed in 2000 at the multiracial Center Club, memory of Emmet Till, battered and killed in Mississippi accused of whistling at a white woman, the sermon preached at the Lincoln Memorial by Martin Luther King in 1963 and his own transfer to a new white school in Baltimore after the

Supreme Court desegregation decision in 1954. That date can mark the new era in Baltimore's history.

5.3. The Jackson Family and Civil Rights

Close to Washington, Baltimore was a strategic battleground of the civil rights movement. The Murphy's, the Marshall's, and the Mitchell's were based in both cities at various times. Although Maryland had been a slave state, it did not leave the Union; Baltimore was a mostly Northern city while still in many ways Southern in that it also contained the fourth largest black population in the country.

A forerunner of the civil rights strategy of the 1960s was the Young People's Form (YPF) led by the young Juanita Jackson in the early 1930s, later the wife of Clarence Mitchell Jr and a lawyer in her own right after graduating from the University of Maryland Law School. Juanita Jackson's mother was Lillie Jackson, the longtime head of the then almost moribund Baltimore chapter of the NAACP. Born Lillie Mae Carroll, she claimed as one ancestor an African chieftain; another Charles Carroll of Carrollton. Deeply religious, she was a fundamentalist opposed to alcohol, tobacco and dancing. Together with her Methodist preacher husband Kieffer Jackson, she built a real estate empire, pressing her black tenants for their rents that she then used for good causes, pressing for results while shouting at both her followers and her enemies. Her family home at 1320 Eutaw Street has recently been restored as a house museum.

The situation was acute during the Depression. In 1932, the long standing black Republican member of the Baltimore City Council lost his seat because of redistricting. A preacher called Kiowa Costonie visiting from Chicago lobbied the local Sanitary Stores and A&P to hire some black clerks; then organized pickets of housewives who marched in front of stores on Pennsylvania Avenue urging blacks to "Buy Where You Can Work." Boycotting and picketing started again in December 1933 just before the Christmas season under the direction of the young lawyer Thurgood Marshall until stopped by an injunction. Although boycotts had gone on before, mass picketing had occurred for the first time. The picketing was found to be effective in reducing patronage and the black community found they had an effective weapon.

Setting a pattern for the 1960s, the YPF was autonomous; based in the local community; more flexible than the larger national organizations like the NAACP or the Urban League. As many as 1000 members of the YPF met every Friday evening at different sites in the four black sections of the city; one night a month for example at the large Bethel A.M.E. Church on Druid Hill Avenue. Speakers such as Walter White of the NAACP and Ralph Bunche from Howard University spoke and then were open for questions from the youthful audience crossing class boundaries in the black community.

The battle moved to the courts; the national NCAAP entered the picture and the local chapter of the NCAAP was re-energized to become eventually the second-largest in the country. The Mitchell and Jackson families as well as Thurgood Marshall became the leaders for the further civil rights battles in Baltimore and on a national level.

Employment opportunities were important, particularly in the midst of a Depression. However, white resistance, including that of unionized labor, made it almost impossible to proceed on behalf of the unskilled and the semi-skilled where the need was greatest and the conflict fiercest. The strategy would remain the same into the 1960s. Education was the key to move beyond jobs as unskilled laborers, domestic servants and laundresses. Like the YPF, the rallying points for energizing the youth would be the black churches and the battleground would now be the courts.

The NAACP long term strategy starting in the 1930s was to use the courts to open educational opportunities to blacks eventually to enter higher skilled jobs. Starting with graduate schools wherein only a few were involved; then to proceed to universities, before engaging the presumably most sensitive and most far reaching issue of the public schools. They felt that segregation would ultimately fall based on the financial cost of separate but truly equal facilities as the minimum required under the law.

5.4. Thurgood Marshall and School Desegregation

The movement in Baltimore toward desegregation would be consistently coordinated with that in nearby Washington DC. National leadership came from the Legal Defense Fund of the NAACP supported by the staff of the Howard University Law School. Thurgood Marshall (christened Thoroughgood after a grandfather who had been a freed slave) was born in segregated Baltimore in 1908. Light-skinned, but proud of their race, both sides of his family ran grocery stores. His paternal grandfather started the business at then still racially mixed West Baltimore at Dolphin and Division Streets to become the city's largest black-owned grocery. One block west was Pennsylvania Avenue, the black Broadway. One block east was Druid Hill Avenue. The latter was the street whose large three-story homes were inhabited by the black professional class where for a time the Marshall family also owned a house. McCulloch Street just one block farther east was the boundary line between the two races.

His maternal grandfather Williams also operated a store but in a white neighborhood. His mother Norma (named after the opera heroine), eventually became an elementary school teacher like her own mother. She went to Maryland's Coppin State College, a segregated teachers' college. His father worked first as a waiter on a dining car on the New York Central out of New York but then as head waiter at the whites-only Maryland Club and then head steward at the posh Gibson Island Club. He never suffered a racial slur without responding and taught his son to do the same and question injustice in the courts.

Young Marshall worked as a dining car waiter on the B&O and later while in law school at the Gibson Island Club as a waiter and bell-hop to put himself through Lincoln University and then Howard University Law School. He graduated with honors in debating from the overcrowded Colored High School in Baltimore. Later named after Frederick Douglass, it was the successor of the Douglass Institute first founded in 1865 by blacks, and then taken over as a public school. It finally received its new far more adequate building in 1925 immediately after Marshall's graduation. Graduates of Baltimore schools like Douglass had a pipeline to Lincoln in southeastern Pennsylvania. Founded in 1854 by a Presbyterian minister; the first degree-granting college for African-American students, its name was changed for the assassinated president. There he once again excelled on the prestigious debating team.

Knowing he was unable because of his race to enter the University of Maryland Law School, Marshall applied to Howard University Law School. Married, he lived with his family in Baltimore and starting in 1930 commuted daily to Washington. Just a year before, Charles Hamilton Houston had become the new Dean of the Law School. A graduate of Amherst and Harvard Law School, Houston created an accredited institution; would become Marshall's mentor and later colleague. He used the law school as a place where budding lawyers would be trained to overcome segregation by being able to prepare cases to the Supreme Court. Graduating first in his class, after a short time trying to practice law in Baltimore as one of the few black attorneys, Marshall was hired in 1936 by his former teacher to join the NCAAP Legal Defense Fund team of lawyers.

Fig. 39 - Thurgood Marshall

Thurgood Marshall was eventually appointed in 1967 by President Lyndon Johnson as the first African-American Associate Justice to the Supreme Court. His statue by the Baltimore sculptor Reuben Kramer stands at the entrance to the Federal Courthouse while his name also adorns the Baltimore International Airport.

The issue of the education of black children in the South was bound up with the entire history of slavery. Education had been denied to blacks during slavery. The story of Frederick Douglass is illustrative. His owner was highly concerned that he had been taught to read. The possibility of freedom was indeed raised in his mind. After Emancipation and the passage of the 13th Amendment, the Freedman's Bureau, in existence only until 1872, had its greatest accomplishment in the building of thousands of schools for black children throughout the South. During the brief period of Reconstruction, public schools, segregated as they were, first received public tax money.

Baltimore had never strongly favored public schools. From the start in the 1820s, public schools were opposed by the elite for sectarian reasons as well as paying for schools they would ordinarily not choose to use. In Baltimore in 1867, the city fired all the Negro teachers when it took over the schools for blacks previously run by private charitable groups. In 1885, a group of Negro ministers first succeeded in having Negro teachers hired for the segregated schools, a process not completed until 1907. No Negro high school existed until the forerunner of the Douglass School opened in 1882.

With the disenfranchisement of blacks in the post-Reconstruction era, tax monies, never plentiful in the South, seldom found their way to improve schools for black children. Literacy tests proved a useful way to disenfranchise black voters. The principle of "separate but equal" facilities on public conveyances reinforced in the 1896 Supreme Court decision in *Plessey vs Ferguson* was enshrined and applied universally, in education as well as in relation to all public accommodation. School expenditures were lower in the South than the North; for black students they were a fraction of the amount spent for whites. The dual system of the South was clearly both separate and unequal.

The National Association for the Advancement of Colored People (NAACP), formed in 1909, hired its first lawyer in 1915 to use the law courts to challenge segregation based on "separate but equal." The initial strategy was to challenge the equality of the schools that were provided; by requiring equality in school expenditures, As early as 1935, in the first case won by Thurgood Marshall. a judge of the Baltimore City Court ordered a black to be admitted to the law school of the University of Maryland.

In response, Maryland funded out-of-state Negro graduate school education but also in-state segregated higher education at a higher level so as to meet the legal criterion of "separate but equal." It founded a college at Bowie and extended state funding to Morgan State, established in the post-Civil War era as Centenary Biblical Institute by the Methodist Conferences of the Mid-Atlantic States. That school's expansion into hilly suburban northeast Baltimore was initially strongly opposed by the white inhabitants of the adjoining area of Lauraville. Once finally achieved, a small suburban area called Morgan Park was also created containing architect-designed homes for the faculty and the local black elite such as W.E.B. DuBois along with entertainers such as Cab Calloway and Eubie Blake.

In 1941, the principle of equal pay was extended to Negro public school teachers throughout Maryland. In 1948 Thurgood Marshall won a case re the University of Oklahoma Law School that "equality, even in regard to physical facilities, never can be achieved…the terms…'separate' and 'equal' cannot be used…there can be no separate equality." In 1950, the effort by the University of Oklahoma to place a black student in an anteroom outside a classroom and be given separate tables in the library was struck down. The time had come to challenge segregation in public schools.

Black schools in Baltimore were clearly unequal. Overcrowded, buildings considered unfit in the 1920s were still in use as schools for colored children in the 1950s. In September 1952, the Baltimore School board decided to admit a dozen Negro students to the elite Polytechnic High School on the premise that "Poly" could not be duplicated in order to meet the criterion of "separate but equal." Then in a unanimous opinion to the credit of then still new Chief Justice Warren, the Supreme Court in 1954 stripped legitimacy from racial segregation in American public education. In the *Brown vs Topeka Board of Education* decision, the Court ruled that "separate educational facilities are inherently unequal." It was in violation of the "equal protection" clause of the 14th Amendment. This was followed immediately with a plan for implementation in the Baltimore public and parochial schools as well as the University of Maryland. By 1957, 26% of black students attended integrated classes.

Baltimore claimed it was in compliance with the Supreme Court by initiating its own system of "freedom of choice" in 1954 immediately after the Supreme Court decision. Actually, the policy served to limit desegregation while also trying to maintain white participation in the partially integrated schools. Most new schools were built in white neighborhoods; no investment was made to overcome the poor quality of the existing schools for colored children over the past ninety years and the overcrowding that had occurred more recently. However, with "white flight," a thousand white students left annually; de facto re-segregation occurred. There was in the 1950s and 1960s a renewal of the process that had gone on throughout the history of Baltimore. In the 1830s and the 1880s, but also in the 1920s, the growth of middle class housing occurred toward the periphery while disinvestment reflecting poverty and disease occurred within the older parts of the city.

The battle shifted to the ballot box. Black political power increased with increased focus on voter registration. In 1954, Harry Cole was the first black elected from Baltimore to the Maryland General Assembly. In 1955, the successful Democratic ticket placed a black Walter Dixon on the Baltimore City Council. In 1958, black candidates were offered by Jack Pollock's Democratic Party organization in the 4th District with two black women elected to the Maryland Assembly.

Pollock's strength in the 4th District had begun to dissipate with the move of his Jewish voter base farther to the northwest. Their concentration in one area due both to restrictive covenants and gerrymandered districts had made them politically conscious and a political force. Pollack had long served as a political boss to be a scapegoat by the *Baltimore Sun* in the name of political purity. His support also dissipated as Jews of the younger generation entered the middle class. By 1968, ten blacks had seats in the Maryland State Assembly. In 1970, Parren Mitchell was elected to Congress, the first ever African-American from Maryland.

5.5. The Mitchell Family and Baltimore Politics

Parren Mitchell was one of seven living children of Clarence Mitchell Sr, a waiter at the Hotel Rennert, one of Baltimore's grandest. According to H.L. Mencken, one of its habitués, it was famous for its black waiters and its Maryland seafood. The Mitchell family lived in a row house they bought in the Harlem Park neighborhood and the children were given the best education then available to blacks. Born in 1922, Parren Mitchell graduated from Frederick Douglass High School before going to the segregated Morgan State College. While fighting in Italy, he was wounded as an officer of the 92nd "Buffalo" Division, the combat unit made up of African Americans from all parts of the country. He sued in 1950 to be able to enroll in the University of Maryland for his master's degree in sociology and was the first African American to graduate. He taught at Morgan State and entered the Civil Rights movement following the example of his elder brother Clarence Mitchell Jr. Parren became the Director of the Community Action Agency (CAP) of "War on Poverty" in Baltimore under President Lyndon Johnson before running for Congress. Re-elected for 9 terms from his 7th District, he led the Black Caucus in the U.S. Congress and ensured minority participation on federal contracts.

Fig. 40 - Parren Mitchell

Clarence Mitchell Jr was born in 1911 and grew up as the eldest in his large family with an ethos of hard work and scrupulous honesty. Both Mitchell brothers helped officiate at services of the St James Episcopal Church whose priest helped found the *Baltimore Afro-American* newspaper. In elementary school, he was taught by the mother of Thurgood Marshall. Like Marshall, he went to Douglass High School, worked alongside him as a waiter at the Gibson Bay Club and went to Lincoln University in Pennsylvania but was unable to graduate for lack of payment for past tuition. After graduation in 1935 from the University of Minnesota, he worked for the Urban League to increase employment opportunities in St Paul. As a reporter for the Baltimore *Afro-American*, he witnessed the aftermath of a lynching in Cambridge Maryland that led to his lifelong commitment to racial justice.

The Director of the National Office of the NAACP in Washington while commuting from Baltimore, his long time work as a lobbyist since 1950 finally came to fruition in accomplishing the great civil rights legislation of the 1960s together with President Lyndon Johnson.

Obscured by the temporarily high birth post-war rate, the population of the city reached its high of 950,000 in the 1950 census. It fell to 900,000 by 1970 with a much higher percentage of blacks. "Blight" equated with black occupancy had been settling over downtown Baltimore during the 1930s and the war years. The decay was extensive in a ring immediately around downtown that was characterized by alley dwellings inhabited by the then 20% of the population that was black prevented from living elsewhere. Over forty-five thousand persons lived in "sub-standard" homes and eighteen thousand in what was considered "dilapidated," lacking indoor toilets or hot water. Schools and recreation facilities were similarly sub-standard. Despite a crash program to enforce sanitary regulations called "The Baltimore Plan," the number of those living in inadequate housing persisted.

Demolition was considered to be the remedy with the homes of the inhabitants of former slums to be replaced ultimately only in part by public housing whose appropriations were constrained by a hostile Congress. The rate of demolition increased. It rose from six hundred units a year in the 1950s to twenty-five hundred in the late 1960s; the number of buildings abandoned for taxes reached one thousand a year. There were five thousand buildings vacant while any new housing appeared in the surrounding white counties.

However, by the 1950s, the role of public housing had changed to exclude those for whom it had been "uplift" out of poverty and the slums. It became a dumping ground for "problem families," primarily for those displaced by the priority given to urban renewal. Whole neighborhoods disappeared that housed low-income persons in favor of highway construction while federal policies favored housing in the suburbs, closed to blacks. By 1965, the population of Baltimore was 40% black; its public housing was over 74% black.

"The Clarence Perkins Homes" are an example of this trajectory. Just east of downtown, they were originally built starting in 1940 as low-rise public housing for working class whites being displaced from that area by slum clearance. To the south, they complemented the black Frederick Douglass Homes to the north. By the time the Perkins Homes were built in 1942, priority under the law was to be given to incoming war workers rather than the displaced Baltimoreans. Social services such as health and recreation were nonetheless placed there preferentially. After the war, the low-income policy was reinstituted with the eviction of those whose income had risen. The emphasis on low-income residents had been an essential selling point to avoid competition with private real estate interests.

Post-war, further public housing could not be easily passed in Congress intent on encouraging home-ownership and opposed to what smacked of socialism. It was supported only to the extent it was connected to slum clearance; moreover, cost considerations took priority over all others. The earlier commitment to high quality design in the tradition of European public housing gave way to barracks-like housing or high rises. Coupled with the fierce opposition encountered in the acquisition of vacant land elsewhere, the answer seemed to be to build high-rise pubic housing in areas where buildings had been cleared.

So it was in Baltimore where the tall Lafayette Courts with over 800 units was built between the two earlier low-rise developments named after Douglass and Perkins. A commitment to "problem families" and the exclusion of those exceeding the income limits created a "housing project" sub-culture. A new slum was created whose intractable problems seemed so great that the only remedy was its planned implosion in 1995 billed as "one of the largest in the Western Hemisphere."

By the end of the 1960s, the distinctions no longer occurred within the boundaries of the city but across political boundaries between the city and adjoining counties. The city could not continue to carry out its role of creating wealth that could support those who were in need. The riots came to Baltimore as they did to hundreds of cities all over America in April 1968 when the two halves "brushed against each other" as they had so many times before in the history of "Mobtown."

The semi-autobiographical story told by Barry Levinson in his film *Avalon* is illustrative. When his Russian Jewish immigrant grandfather arrived in 1914, he found America a country full of exciting lights exemplified by the 4th of July and Baltimore "such a beautiful place." The story is told of family life in the pre-war and early post-World War II decades in the "Nederland" of two story row houses in closer-in West Baltimore complete with porches and a small front yard and close family connections.

The story is then of the move in the flush of post-World War II prosperity to the higher ground of the more affluent "suburbs" with their detached houses and green lawns to an area in northwest known as Forest Park, still within the city limits. It was where Levinson himself attended high school and told in one of his movies of the school integration that began in a tentative fashion in the fall of 1954. Others also recall fifty-years later the momentous change that their lives underwent with the first three African American students that entered their second grade class in P.S. 69 in Forest Park.

However, Levinson documents in his movie *Avalon* how the move to the suburbs coincided with the break up of extended family relationships as well as their sense of neighborhood. The changes were further precipitated by the mugging in the old neighborhood of the young first generation door-to-door "installment salesman," an occurrence unheard of by the older generation in their own lives. By the end of the movie in the 1970s, the grandfather spoke of not only the destruction of the family's earlier row house with porch in their legendary Northwest Baltimore but that their very earliest old immigrant neighborhood in East Baltimore no longer existed. The immigrant American Dream had burned and turned to ashes.

One of the unexpected outcomes of these turbulent times was the rise to national notice in 1968 of Spiro Agnew, the Governor of Maryland. The County Executive of Baltimore County, he appeared to be the triumph of modernity over old-style politics, the ultimate suburbanite and the candidate of the PTAs and the Kiwanis clubs. He was elected to the office of governor in 1966 as a relatively liberal alternative to the openly racist platform of the Democratic candidate George Mahoney. The latter's campaign motto "A Man's Home is His Castle – Protect It" did not require translation in this era surrounding the passage of "Open Housing," last of the major Civil Rights Bills of the 1960s.

The Civil Rights Bill of 1968 ended federal support for discrimination in housing in the overwhelming majority of units for sale or rental. It followed the Civil Rights bill of 1964 that assured equal accommodation and the Civil Rights Bill of 1965 that assured voting rights. The Southern Democrats had already begun to move out of the Democratic Party. Urban riots and expressions of "Black Power" alienated many whites. "Open housing" and "law and order" were the issues that eventually split the New Deal Democratic Party coalition. The election of Richard Nixon and Spiro Agnew in 1968 was the beginning of both the "Suburban Strategy" and the "Southern Strategy" that helped establish the national hegemony of the Republican Party for the next generation by stirring up racial animosities.

5.6. Spiro Agnew and the Southern Strategy

Fig. 41 - Spiro Agnew

Spiro Agnew gained national notice for the first time in late March 1968 when he dealt strongly with students at the largely black Bowie State University. He refused to meet with them on campus to address their complaints and had them arrested when they "sat in" at the Maryland State Capitol; he then abruptly closed the university. A short time later, in the context of the riot in early April 1968 following the assassination of Martin Luther King, surrounded by the state military leaders, he confronted a delegation of Baltimore's black community leaders he had invited. In an accusatory tone, he described them as tools of Stokely Carmichael and other extremists. He confronted and denigrated the moderates who had tried to restore order on the streets such as Clarence Mitchell III, a state senator, and his mother Juanita Jackson Mitchell the NAACP leader, considered to be like the Kennedy's in their role in the black community.

Spiro Theodore Agnew's own sources was in the Greek immigrant community of Baltimore; moreover, his transition to the suburbs can help explain his unexpected selection as vice-president in the "law and order" 1968 Nixon campaign. He was born in a second floor rear apartment at the corner of Madison and Howard Streets in West Baltimore in 1918. In the Greek tradition, the name given to the only son of Theodofrastos Spiro Angnostopoulos reversed that of his father.

The father operated a small restaurant farther down Howard Street and then a larger one that enabled the family to move to solidly middle class Forest Park. Later, having apparently lost the restaurant during the Depression, the senior Agnew, without complaint, carried on the physically taxing job of delivering produce from the market to restaurants. From a non-Greek background, his mother was a widow with a son of her own when she married a Greek immigrant. A serious man and a strict disciplinarian, with his Greek accent, his father would read philosophy and discuss politics with his son rather than sports. He instilled the fierce pride and orderliness in one's thinking as well as his impeccable appearance that would characterize his son's personal characteristics. These characteristics would also affect his almost visceral response to those who opposed him, seeming to bring disorder into his life.

Shy young Agnew attended co-ed Forest Park High School in the 1930s, then one of the city's better high schools but not the best academically. He left no notice of any achievements in his 1937 senior yearbook. Enrolled for a time at Johns Hopkins University, financial problems and lack of ongoing interest in his chemistry curriculum led to his withdrawal. He worked as a junior underwriter at the Maryland Casualty Company and earned a barely creditable record at night school at the then still unaccredited University of Baltimore Law School.

Drafted into the army, he became an officer eventually attached to the 54th Armored Infantry Battalion in France, fought at the Battle of the Bulge and then in Germany for which he received the Bronze Star but no promotion. More focused on his studies on his return, married and with children, he passed the bar. After a series of low level legal jobs, he finally started his own firm with labor unions as well as a black fishing cooperative as his main clientele.

Agnew moved his law practice in 1955 to Towson, the booming county seat of suburban Baltimore County where he rose in politics via the local PTA and then the Kiwanis Club of his neo-colonial row house community of Loch Raven. Even when a national political figure, he and his wife continued to meet monthly on Saturday night with couples that had been their neighbors in Loch Raven.

A registered Republican in a majority Democratic area, he entered local politics on behalf of a charter government that took power away from the traditional Democratic Party county commissioners. In the post-World War II era, the new suburbanites were dissatisfied with the old-line County Commissioner form of government ruled since 1938 by figures such as Christian Kahl and Michael Birmingham. The old-boy network permitted unbridled development while adhering to a policy of low taxes and inexpensive services. In 1956, Baltimore County followed Montgomery County near Washington in establishing "charter rule" that provided for greater self-government.

After gaining a reputation for honesty (later found to be undeserved) in his role on the county zoning appeals board during a period of great growth, Agnew stood successfully as a reform-minded minority Republican against the establishment as County Executive in 1962. Looked upon as mildly progressive, his personal meticulousness and legalism ultimately reflected his suburban white community. That community defined itself as antithetical to the "inner city" characterized as being one of anarchy and disease.

Whenever confronted by mass picketing such as at the amusement park at Gwynn Oaks he considered illegal or any other tactic he considered to be pressuring him, Agnew's response was to become angry and resist.

Nevertheless, in the context of the "white backlash" represented by heavy vote in Maryland for George Wallace and John Birch Society members in 1964, if "by your enemies shall you be known," Agnew seemed to be reasonably liberal. Although opposed to "open housing" for individual owners, as Baltimore County Executive he would allow opening up larger new housing developments.

The Democratic majority of Maryland was split in the primary. George Mahoney had failed when he had run for office many times before. There was a large field of candidates in the Democratic primary; only Mahoney was the one clearly opposed to open housing. In 1966, his basic cadre of 100,000 voters was enough to gain him the Democratic Party nomination, usually tantamount to election in this normally Democratic state. However, the selection of George Mahoney based on an appeal against open housing split the Democratic majority. Liberal voters in Montgomery County and elsewhere voted Republican. Spiro Agnew was elected governor and Marvin Mandel was elected by the legislature as his replacement. The rest is history far beyond the confines of Maryland.

Agnew became the most controversial abrasive vice-president in American history. In 1972, Maryland re-elected the Nixon-Agnew ticket over McGovern by over 400,000 votes. Despite Agnew's political prominence in 1972 after being the Nixon hatchet man during the first term and his massive re-election along with President Nixon, they were both eventually forced to resign. Agnew was the first to go because of bribery and corruption that had continued since the onset of his career in Maryland. He was replaced as vice-president by Gerald Ford who then actually acceded to the presidency after Watergate.

5.7. Marvin Mandel and Maryland Politics

Marvin Mandel was born in the Pimlico area the son of a poor Jewish garment worker and sometime union organizer who, due to poor health, opened a neighborhood liquor store. He sold newspapers at the Pimlico Race Track and, only five foot-six, became a boxer. He met his wife, from a more affluent family, while in high school. After high school for the college-bound at Baltimore City College, he enrolled at University of Maryland on his family's shoestring. After two years mainly devoted to fraternity life, he left. He answered a draft call in 1942 after graduating from the University of Maryland Law School.

A non-commissioned officer, he taught riflery and then after the war went into the practice of law. Always living modestly, he lived in rental housing in an apartment on Upper Park Heights Avenue. His clientele came mainly from the Block, the seedy area of Baltimore Street devoted to bars and prostitutes. Affable and retiring, politics was his real passion. He joined Jack Pollack's organization in the 4th district and was elected to the General Assembly in 1952.

Ever ready to bring antagonists together "to make the system work," he was chosen as chair of the Baltimore City delegation to the General Assembly and then Chair of the important Ways and Means Committee in 1953. After winning re-election many times with Pollack's support, he ran in opposition and gained a reputation as a "giant-killer."

Appointed Speaker of the Maryland lower house in 1962, his role as Speaker fitted him well. He worked the levers of power to bring about a great legislative record for the Governor Willard Tawes.

Fig. 42 - Marvin Mandel

He met beautiful blonde Jeanne Dorsey, the wife of a state senator from St Mary's County. Their love affair went on even as he became governor by vote of the Assembly in 1968; was elected in 1970 after having achieved spectacular legislative triumphs; and then once more in 1974. Government reorganization made Maryland a model for the nation. Under Mandel, the state was in the forefront of progressive causes from abortion to mass transit and consumer protection. He is credited with insuring the passage of the first leg of the long-planned Metro through northwest Baltimore. Nevertheless, he came under scrutiny for possible ethics violation by the *Baltimore Sun* and the *Washington Post*, suspicious of his connections and secretive mode of operation.

In the background was Irving Kovens, Mandel's fund raiser who insured raising money for elections but also for dealing with his embarrassing divorce and a punitive settlement. It seemed fitting to Marvin Mandel and Jeanne Dorsey to marry in time for her to come into the open to assume a role as First Lady of Maryland displacing his outraged long time wife. To marry Jeanne was one of the few non-political decisions he had ever made and became his political undoing. The suspected source for financing that divorce settlement by Kovens became Mandel's nemesis and led to his conviction of bribery under the excessively broad rubric of "mail fraud."

Highway planning had been a priority since the passage if the Interstate Highway Act of 1956 provided federal funds for road building. At various times since the 1940s, an east-west expressway has been planned to cross the city of Baltimore. Now in the 1960s, a road was to unite with the Baltimore Beltway to prevent a bypass of the city by interstate traffic. To avoid the more genteel districts of upper Charles Street, the decision was to swing the new road to the south through Canton and Fells Point while also serving downtown. The area had already become blighted by the previously aborted plans since the 1940s for an east-west expressway. On the west, the road would go through Leakin Park adjoining Gwynn's Falls but also take more housing occupied by the black community of Rosemount. The building of the Baltimore Harbor Tunnel ended the immediate need for a solution to the very inadequate requirement for interstate traffic to cross Baltimore on Rte 40. The plans for the east-west expressway remained on the drawing board.

5.8. Barbara Mikulski and the New Democratic Coalition

Born in 1936, Barbara Mikuski was the eldest of three daughters of a Polish family that owned a grocery store in Highlandtown. Her grandparents' Polish bakery on Eastern Avenue was particularly well known. A blue collar neighborhood of row houses in Southeast Baltimore, it had first been settled by Germans immediately after the Civil War with its first church built by the Redemptorist Fathers in 1872 on the hill that was the original site of a Union fort, hence the name of Highland Town.

Fig. 43 - Barbara Mikulski

Southeast Baltimore has been since successively settled by Poles, Czechs, Lithuanians and Greeks. Getting off the ships at Locust Point, they had been ferried to Fell's Point before migrating all the way—thirty blocks—to what seemed like another world in Highland Town with its row houses and white marble steps to be maintained by the householder laid out by the Canton Company offering houses for as little as $480. Noted for its breweries and slaughterhouses as well as its high rate of home ownership, it was not annexed to the city until 1918. There still remained the ethnic taverns on each corner where the men could each find their tribal atmosphere on endless streets of two-story narrow row-houses interspersed by stone churches at the corners.

On a hill just east of Patterson Park, Highlandtown is bound on the north by East Lombard Street and on the south by the commercial strip of Eastern Avenue where the shop owners and their families lived above the store; on the west by Highlandtown Avenue and the east by South Haven Street. The men could take the subsidized streetcar on Eastern Avenue to work in the steel mills of Sparrows Point where, after the passage of the Wagner Act in 1935, they helped organize the steelworkers union.

Barbara Mikulski worked in the family grocery store after school while enrolled in the Institute of Notre Dame. She speaks of her father carrying his customers during their strike against Bethlehem Steel at Sparrow's Point. She also speaks of the Jewish wholesale grocer Joffe Brothers carrying her father after he was wiped out by a fire. Thinking about becoming a nun, she realized she was too rebellious to accept the discipline of a religious order and too emotionally raw to traipse sweetly among a gentle flock.

Taught by the nuns to "Love Thy Neighbor," she did the next best thing and became a social worker. She received her degree at Mount St Agnes College then in Mount Washington (now part of Loyola University) and the MSW from University of Maryland. One of her first jobs after graduation was to establish in the black Catholic parish of St Francis Xavier a program for drug abuse counseling. She was part of a more general effort led by Cardinal Shehan to address long dormant issues of racial justice that were opposed by many Catholic laypersons. Working on health access issues with the elderly and the poor for Catholic Charities and then for the City of Baltimore, she also became a sociology professor at Loyola College.

Under the auspices of the Office of Economic Opportunity as part of President Johnson's "War on Poverty," Barbara Mikulski organized opposition to the building of the east-west expressway across Fells Point and Federal Hill. The rejection considered Baltimore's "finest hour." I-95 was eventually routed farther south across south Baltimore. However, the need for an east-west transportation link remains; it now is planned as the new "red line" of the still incomplete Baltimore Metro. The Jones Falls Expressway remains the only link from the interstate highway system into downtown.

Barbara Mikulski first received national notice with a speech in 1970 at a conference at Catholic University of America and an op-ed piece in the New York Times dealing with the needs of the "ethnics" that she has continued to represent in the national arena. She grew up in a place where neighbors did help each other; they were all related to the same origins, the same culture. When the downtown banks would not finance mortgages, the Poles established their own Savings & Loans on Eastern Avenue, on what Barbara Mikulski called "the Polish Wall Street." One of Baltimore's three Polish "national parishes" was local parish of St Casmir's founded in the early 1900s as an outgrowth of the earlier St Stanislaus in Fell's Point. That culture was not necessarily bigoted against blacks. Yet, in the aftermath of the 1968 riots, there was a mass exodus that threatened to destroy the Baltimore she had known of neighborhoods but were now no longer made up of all the same people.

Elected to the Baltimore City Council in 1971 as an independent candidate, she entered Congress from the overwhelmingly Democratic 3rd District in 1976 and the U.S. Senate in 1986. She lived until very recently in Baltimore's Fell's Point. Now living on upper Charles Street, she still commutes to Washington and may still attend the Polish language early mass at her church. One of the leading women in the Senate, she has led in improving women's health and in endorsing then Senator Hillary Clinton for president in 2007. She has continued to speak on health issues and has contributed her very forthright and formidable voice to the new Democratic Party coalition that elected President Barak Obama in 2008 and 2012.

CHAPTER 6
THE BALTIMORE RENAISSANCE
1975-

6.1 A Regional City

The city's population fell precipitously following 1970 to reach less than 800,000, with an even greater fall in median income. The population of Baltimore County continued to rise as that of the city fell. The big jump occurred during the 1970s, reaching a regional population within the city and six adjoining counties approximating 2,500,000 by the year 2000, with but one quarter living in the city. Baltimore has indeed become a region crossing artificial political boundaries.

The riots of 1968 became a keystone of the "law and order" stance of the Republican Party with Spiro Agnew the unlikely fountainhead and Baltimore the symbol of decay. The closing in 1973 of the Flower Mart that had been an annual event in Mount Vernon Place since 1911 was a mark that Baltimore no longer seemed to have a stable future. However, that same year, the Baltimore City Fair moved its venue from the safer precincts of Charles Center to the Inner Harbor.

The riots of Holy Week 1968 after the assassination of Martin Luther King Jr broke out in Baltimore on April 6th, two days later. The financial losses in Baltimore were second only to those in Washington DC. Six lives were lost. It started in the heart of East Baltimore at North Gay and North Avenue on a Saturday night, spilling over farther north onto Harford Road and Guilford Avenue, then to other neighborhoods throughout the city most particularly Pennsylvania Avenue in West Baltimore. The original source of the riot was in an area that had long been slated for demolition in order to build a highway despite long term opposition by those living there. Still in 2013 characterized by blocks of boarded up row houses, there is some evidence of newly painted buildings opposite the massive Board of Education complex.

Governor Agnew declared a state of emergency by 8 PM and instituted a curfew. By 4 AM on April 7th, 300 fires had erupted. By April 9th, calm had returned to the extent that the Baltimore Orioles played their opening game just a day late on April 10th. Agnew treated the riots as a criminal matter. His and others' use of the riots for national political ends brought about long continued reverberations.

"Urban renewal" in the manner of "One Charles Center" was the hope of the future with a theater, exhibition center, offices and apartments. The founding of the "Center Club" in 1962 on the roof of Charles Center was part of this new initiative and helped the building attract prestigious tenants. For the first time in Baltimore history, a luncheon club was founded whose membership was not to be affected by the applicant's racial or ethnic identity. There was a mixed board that included Joseph Meyerhoff as vice-president and others who were of the Baltimore establishment, some who were members of the then still highly restrictive Maryland Club. The clubhouse of the latter still stands at the corner of North Charles and Eager Streets in the neighborhood of the Belvedere Hotel. Its turn of the century oak paneled building is filled with a collection of its members' hunting trophies.

The Charles Center was built by private interests on land acquired cheaply by eminent domain with government offices enhancing the rental rolls. It was unique to Baltimore by incorporating contemporary modernist buildings into the design. Designed by Mies Van der Rohe, one of the great masters of the International Style, One Charles Center reflects the classical purity of that style and that architect's devotion to exacting standards. The adjacent competing Blaustein Building was designed by a fellow Bauhaus veteran Marcel Breuer. The Blaustein family, wealthy based upon their petroleum holdings, was active in Jewish community organizations on a national level.

Other later buildings that make up the Charles Center were more decorative. Nevertheless, the development went into default in the next decades when CSX Railroad, having absorbed the B&O, moved its headquarters elsewhere. Several of the longtime local banks and financiers such as Alexander Brown & Company and even the quintessential *Baltimore Sun* were bought by larger companies elsewhere. They cut employees and moved their headquarters and decision making out of Baltimore. From 1970 to 1985, industrial employment continued to fall in half.

Although many attributed the changes of the 1970s and beyond to the riots of April 1968, the effects were more nuanced and not as directly related as usually thought. For example, the almost total disappearance of the former Jewish shopping district of East Lombard Street was not due to the riots per se; physical damage was actually minimal. Stores reopened but fewer whites came to shop from elsewhere. When the street was closed for almost a year in 1976 by urban renewal road repair, half the remaining stores closed; an action aided by the growth of malls. The Flaghouse Court housing that adjoined the street became not only entirely black but a war zone in the 1980s characterized by guns and drugs that led to its demolition in the 1990s.

What had been in the 1940s known as "Row House City," frequently owner-occupied, had been eviscerated by the 1980s. The term "hollowed out" is frequently used. As the housing disappeared to be replaced by vacant houses and then vacant land, the tax base also disappeared. Since families with children moved out because of poor schools, only single persons and the elderly remained behind along with the poorer blacks needing services that could no longer be afforded even with federal and state grants. Middle-class blacks joined the exodus as suburban racial barriers fell. Owner-occupied housing declined. Employment, no longer in unionized well-paid manufacturing and trade for the semi-skilled, was in education and health care for the more highly skilled for which the educational system frequently failed to prepare the underclass.

Despite improvement in the dock facilities and commitment to containerization, Baltimore scarcely held its own as a commercial port. Exports such as grain shipments went preferentially through the St Lawrence Seaway, coal went out from Hampton Roads. Imports did rise of foreign-made cars, particularly from Japan. Jobs in the port declined significantly with mechanization and containerization. There had once been five separate hiring halls for the longshoremen at Locust Point with two locals for stevedores, one for blacks, another for whites. The very few members of the union now work only a few hours each week with the limited work that is still available claimed by nepotism, with incomes even more supplemented by thievery. The need was felt for rejuvenation of the waterfront.

6.2. James Rouse and Harbor Place

James Rouse was the leading real estate developer of the post-World War II era with particular influence on the Baltimore area. Born in Easton Maryland in Talbot County in 1914, he surmounted family financial difficulties that prevented him from finishing his undergraduate schooling at the University of Virginia. He came to Baltimore in 1933, worked long hours as a garage attendant while completing law school at the University of Maryland. He began his career in mortgage housing during the 1930s under the auspices of the Federal Housing Authority and then in the post-World War II era built some of the country's early shopping malls in the Baltimore area. His Mondawmin Mall was innovative with its ornamental fountains; his Harundale Mall was the first to be enclosed.

Fig. 44 - James Rouse

In the 1960s, he built within Baltimore City at Falls Road and Northern Parkway and Cold Spring Lane "Cross Keys," the first of his planned communities. It took its name from the inn that stood at the crossroads of Falls Road and Cold Spring Lane on part of the grounds of the former golf course of the Baltimore Country Club, which in turn had been the site of a historic African-American community. Designed in part by the then unknown Frank Gehry, overall it foreshadowed later developments by having a town center, pedestrian walkways and a variety of housing types. Cross Keys was followed in the same spirit by the much larger city of Columbia between Washington and Baltimore in Howard County that Rouse bravely stated was free of racial, religious or economic discrimination.

Rouse's greatest impact has been the building "festival sites" in cities such as Boston's Faneuil Hall Marketplace, New York's South Street Seaport and Baltimore's Harbor Place on the Inner Harbor as exemplars of urban regeneration. The old waterfront was replaced by a Convention Center surrounded by hotels, pavilions selling crafts and restaurants for tourists. Rouse insisted that the economic gains also encompass issues of quality of life, of bringing people together as a community.

The availability of federal monies coupled with the political will of William Donald Schaefer during the 1970s brought about this much vaunted "Baltimore Renaissance."

6.3. William Donald Schaefer and Charm City

When H. L. Mencken lived in Baltimore, he considered it "a city of charm." By the time William Donald Shafer became mayor in 1971, he was reduced to having people collect "charms" to form a bracelet to fulfill that sobriquet. In light of the urban decay, the name became for many a cruel joke that Schaefer tried mightily to overcome.

Fig. 45 - William Donald Schaefer

Consistent with the process followed by Charles Center, there was a mixture of public and private money to renew the lowest portion of the old city. With the availability of federal money in block grants to cities, Schaefer could devote large sums to the urban renewal projects of Inner Harbor including the centerpiece of Harbor Place with its shops and restaurants and festival air as well as hotels and convention center. The extraordinarily attractive National Aquarium and the Maryland Science Center completed the surroundings of the Inner Harbor.

William Donald Schaefer was born in Baltimore in 1921, grew up in the Edmondson Village section in West Baltimore, went to all-boys Baltimore City College High School, America's third-oldest and cross town rival of Poly, and the University of Baltimore Law School.

A hospital administrator in the U.S. Army during World War II, he entered law practice as a real estate lawyer. Unmarried, he lived throughout his career in Baltimore with his mother in a modest row house in West Baltimore until moving to the Governor's Mansion in Annapolis at age sixty-five.

Schaefer entered politics via the Allendale-Lyndhurst Neighborhood Association and based both his political career and his program subsequent to his election on such associations. Multi-purpose centers, health clinics, and senior centers were all built in the neighborhoods to strengthen them and stabilize their deterioration. Yet his own neighborhood, all-white in the 1950s, became all-black when, in the wake of the planned east-west highway, services declined.

Elected to the Baltimore City Council in 1955 from the 5th district with "machine support," he was elected Chair of the City Council in 1967 on his own and mayor in 1971. He focused on building pride in the city by boosterism like his charm bracelet campaign. Re-elected by overwhelming majorities for a total of four terms; in recognition of the changing demography, he chose the first black police commissioner for a department traditionally Irish and Italian. Yet despite all efforts, the schools continued to deteriorate.

With the departure of industry such as Bethlehem Steel and General Motors, Schaefer's dream to replace the city's economic base with tourism seemed to be realized by the success of "Harbor Place." Concomitant was a focus on the elation engendered by the success of the major league Orioles baseball team and the NFL teams of the

Colts and then the Ravens. The last was brought to Baltimore from Cleveland with the active involvement of Schaefer when the Colts left under threat of increased taxation. The attractive Camden Yards Oriole Baseball Stadium and the adjacent M&T Football Stadium replaced the old Memorial Stadium. Baltimore finally could claim its proper role as a major league city under William Schaefer!

The story of Edmondson Village in West Baltimore, Schaefer's home area, exemplifies the history of several of the other street car suburbs. Some three miles from downtown, it was the child of James Keelty, an Irish immigrant. Starting in 1916, he built hundreds of row houses with porches and then one-car garages for lower middle class families clustered around St Bernadine's Church, named after his dead daughter. The area streetcar ran on the line of Edmondson Avenue crossing Gwynn's Falls up to the uplands on the border of the 1888 boundary. On the border was the country estate of Mary Frick Garrett Jacobs called "Uplands" she had inherited from her father.

The Ellicott City Streetcar line that ran on Edmondson Road began service in 1899; a new concrete arch bridge was completed in 1910 across Gwynn's Falls. From 1910 to 1930, the population of Edmondson Village rose from 100 to nearly 9,000 with the building of one-family "daylight" row houses, broader than they were deep as compared to the earlier west side pattern. They were 20-22 feet wide and 35 feet deep compared to the earlier 15 foot width and 40 foot depth. This enabled each room to have at least one window.

In 1947, Joseph Meyerhoff built his first regional shopping center on Edmondson Road with a Colonial Williamsburg motif and branch of Hothschild-Kohn downtown department store. In 1954, immediately after the Supreme Court desegregation decision, suddenly the Keelty Company sold all its yet un-built upon land and moved its operations to Baltimore County where the number of housing units being built exceeded for the first time that of the city. With little owner turnover, the neighborhood lacked young children to fill its schools. When owners died, their houses became available. Real estate "blockbusters" moved in.

With the desegregation of the schools, black students began to appear in the local junior high school and black families moved in to be close to the school. Yet blacks were still not permitted to try on clothing or were otherwise served in the Edmondson Village Shopping Center. In the 1960s, racial barriers fell in the stores. But Westview Mall, just a mile away in the County near the Beltway exchange, also built by the Meyerhoff Company in 1958, was where white shoppers went. The Edmondson Village Shopping Center stores began to deteriorate even before the neighborhood became all-black.

The Baltimore School Board ended segregated schools soon after the 1954 Supreme Court decision in 1954. "Freedom of choice" enabled black students to transfer to schools of their choice but priority was still given to neighborhood children so that segregated residential patterns in large part still held. Responsibility for racial mixing was thus based on families who wished to transport their children to school. For example in the first flush of desegregation, black students enrolled at South Baltimore High School at Federal Hill met with strong opposition; discouraged, their siblings fell back to black-majority schools like Douglass, now in the former old campus of Western High School near Coppin State. Mixing did occasionally occur of young men hanging out to play ball.

Although moderate racial mixing occurred in white schools, no white would choose to go to a black school in dilapidated buildings taught by poorly trained black teachers. Soon the entire school district became majority black with re-segregation as each school became successively black following de facto segregation of housing patterns. The *Sunpapers* continued to list classified and real estate ads as well as news stories with racial designations that encouraged continued re-segregation during the 1950s and early 1960s. By 1962, there were no multi-racial apartment complexes.

With the renewal of the Civil Rights Movement in 1963, a group of parents and the NAACP sued to create true "freedom of choice." However, with "blockbusting," housing re-segregation proceeded with even greater exodus of white students from the Baltimore schools. Thomas D'Alessandro III, a liberal son of Little Italy, was elected mayor in 1967 on a platform of bi-racial cooperation and school improvement. He took office just before the riots of April 1968. The riots justified white fears of black violence, particularly by Jewish business owners. Black moderate leaders, pressed by the young for the need for black solidarity, were being tarred by some with the same brush as those who were truly militant.

Various superintendants came and went, white and black. Despite construction of new schools, nothing seemed to work to end segregation per se. By 1974, federal orders to desegregate that would require busing were actively opposed by whites in Southeastern Baltimore, in the area of Canton and Highland Town. Although integration was the law, it could not be enforced by the courts or even by the Cardinal Archbishop; nor could Baltimore do more than it had. There would be no busing across county lines. The problem remained as to how to raise the quality of the schools, integrated or not; but now to be under black control. Planned or unplanned, shrinkage of the city became accepted policy with withdrawal of city services with the idea that cities are considered obsolete, to be recycled.

By the 1980s, Baltimore had the dubious rating of being the second worst-off large city in the country as measured by its low percentage of high school graduates reflecting somewhat the 15% decline in school expenditures; a high poverty level with an infant mortality comparable to Mexico reflecting a 45% decline in social expenditures.

6.4. Kurt Schmoke and Baltimore Politics

Kurt Schmoke seemed to be a last hope. Born in Baltimore in 1949, his father was a chemist in the U.S. Army and his mother Irene a social worker and a colleague of Barbara Mikulski. He was enrolled at the intensive classical curriculum at Baltimore City College High School where he was also the star football player before going to

Yale. A Rhodes Scholar at Oxford, he graduated from the Harvard Law School. A member of a prestigious downtown Baltimore law firm, he had also been an official in the Jimmy Carter White House. Elected Baltimore States Attorney in 1982, he ran for mayor in 1987. He narrowly defeated the black interim mayor in his first crucial Democratic primary election, a man who had been a protégé of William Schaefer when the latter became governor. Schmoke was elected for a total of three terms, the first black mayor elected in Baltimore's history.

Fig. 46 - Kurt Schmoke

Acclaimed as the representative of the new generation of black politicians, Schmoke was seemingly the best of what Baltimore had to offer. His tenure was associated with incremental improvements in public housing and literacy. He was however unsuccessful in overcoming, even by his controversial advocacy for the decriminalization of drugs, the plague caused by drugs in Baltimore's public housing. After leaving the mayoralty, he moved to Washington to become Dean of the Howard University Law School.

Despite all the efforts and the court rulings, Thurgood Marshall's sad prediction of two cities—one black, one white- holds true to a great degree. One can no longer consider Baltimore city as a sole entity; it must be considered but a part of its larger region that crosses artificial political boundaries. Most neighborhoods in the Baltimore region are still racially segregated; sorting by race, religion and income remains more rigorous than in many other American cities.

Public housing, the perennial hope since the 1930s for removing blight, rather concentrated and amplified blight in both high and low rise buildings. Their demolition has occurred but the diffusion of their inhabitants is considered politically impossible. Infection rates in poor areas exceed that elsewhere with AIDS replacing the TB and typhoid of the earlier eras; with hepatitis in train with addiction. Yet its world class educational institutions and hospitals and its grittiness as well as its still attractive architecture offer hope for its future.

Early in the post-war era, the large tracts of housing built for war workers in Dundalk in eastern Baltimore County formed the model for thousands of small houses for returning veterans, with no money down throughout Baltimore County. The rise of the automobile and the commitment to the development of private detached housing in the post-World War II led to the development of roads that no longer connected the suburbs only to downtown Baltimore. Lateral roads such as Northern Parkway and Cold Spring Lane permitted a northern bypass that culminated in the development of the Baltimore Beltway in the 1960s.

Throughout the 19th century, Baltimore County, long rural and agricultural, was dependent on the railroads serving Baltimore City for the industrial development that did occur such as quarrying of marble near Cockeysville and granite from a town of the same name near Randallstown. Papermaking was a major industry in the northern part of the county where there was abundant clear water near Beckleysville. Owing's Mill ground wheat to make flour until the water supply lessened; the Union Manufacturing Company's textile mills rose again in the 1880s as the "Oella Mills" when bought by William J. Dickey to manufacture woolen cloth. Trains also carried passengers to such resorts as Green Springs whose name remains on a prominent road.

The earliest development of suburban housing in the county depended on the development of the horse car and then electric railways. In the 1860s, one horse car line ran west along the Frederick Turnpike to Catonsville; another along the York Road to Towson. The population of the county reached 60,000 in the 1870s augmented by summer houses of Baltimoreans. A line along the Harford Road appeared in the 1870s. Even farther east in Baltimore County, Essex had a streetcar line from Baltimore inducing some of Canton's German residents to move there, particularly after a steel rolling mill was built. The Back River Sewage Plant provided a counter force to development.

The Baltimore, Pimlico and Pikesville Railway used electric power in the early 1890s and, as the Baltimore and Northern, gained entry below North Avenue into Baltimore city along the Falls Turnpike, down Charles and Calvert Streets to terminate at Baltimore Street. It brought fairgoers to the Pimlico one-mile race track that started in 1870 in an area that had held the Maryland State Fair. The major east-west Rogers Avenue is named after the designer of the race course. Also, the site of the Electric Amusement Park in the 1890s, until the post-war exodus beyond the county line, it was the strip shopping area of those living on the edges of Upper Park Heights Avenue with the local bank, branch library and movie house.

Lutherville near Towson was one of the earliest incorporated suburban towns, named after the religious affiliation of its sponsors and the Lutherville Female Seminary (later the Maryland College for Young Ladies) that was its focus. The Towson family farm at the crossroads of the York and Joppa Roads became in 1790 part of the site of "Hampton" built by Charles Ridgely. The land was noted for its marble and limestone deposits as well as iron ore. The Ridgely fortune, largely based on ironworks, was augmented during the Revolutionary War by confiscated Loyalist properties. In the next generation, John Ridgely in turn conveyed a large parcel to Henry Chew on occasion of marriage to his daughter Harriet that would be a large part of the land upon which modern day Towson is built.

Prior to the 1850s, Baltimore County shared the cost and occupancy of its public buildings with the city of Baltimore; in 1854, they separated and **Towson** was established as the county seat with the county courthouse completed in 1857. Towson's inhabitants welcomed native son Harry Gilmor as he led a Confederate cavalry raid into Maryland in July 1864. One of the most daring of the partisan raiders, Gilmor commanded the 1st and 2nd Maryland Confederate Cavalry put under the overall command of another fellow Marylander Brigadier General George H Steuart, a large landholder in West Baltimore

The substantial number of former slaves from the Ridgely plantation settled mainly in East Towson with their first school opened under Freedmen's Bureau auspices in 1867. St James A.M.E. Church was founded in 1861 and opened its own first building in 1881. During a short period in 1870, the town was incorporated and the blacks, newly enfranchised by the 15th Amendment, chose to exercise their right to vote. In response, the town ceased to be incorporated until well into the 20th century in an effort by the county commissioners to disenfranchise the black voters of East Towson.

Mainly a summer colony, Towson remained a sleepy town until the 1890s when the electric railways brought the beginnings of substantial suburban development at Aigburth Vale. There was a Second Empire mansion complete with mansard roof, designed by the Baltimore firm of Niernsee and Neilson. The owner was John E. Owens, the most famous American comedic actor. His best known role was as "Solon Shingle" in the *People's Lawyer*. He also traded on his ineptness as a gentleman farmer in reference to his farm at Aigburth Vale. He is also credited with making the old minstrel tune "Dixie" well known at a show in New Orleans on the eve of the Civil War, leading to its adoption as a Confederate anthem.

After the death of Owens in the 1880s, the house became a summer boarding house while the acreage became building lots. During the 20th century, it was operated as a psychiatric facility by Dr and Mrs Sargent for patients discharged from the Shepherd Pratt Hospital. Left to the Board of Education, it deteriorated in their hands and it was finally converted into housing for the elderly. Towson has grown to form a complex of office towers along with hotels on the ridge between the campus of Towson State University to the south along York Road and the rustic acres of Goucher College on the north.

The village of **Ruxton** between Charles Street on the east and Falls Road in the west lies within the modern Towson census tract. It derives its name from one of its early 19th century owners in what was originally called Back River-Upper Hundred. Nicholas Ruxton Moore received a large bequest from his uncle Nicholas Ruxton Gay, recognized as one of Baltimore's early street commissioners by Gay Street. The nephew, eventually a captain in the Maryland Light Dragoons in the Yorktown Campaign in 1781, settled his family on a farm he had bought in upper Baltimore County in 1794. Elected to Congress in 1803 as a Jeffersonian, he served until 1816. In the 1880s, the estate called Rolandvue was subdivided and referred to as Ruxton for the first time, to be served by the Northern Central Railroad. Ruxton Heights and Riderwood followed in the early 20th century when Roland Park was also being developed by house lots.

The land on which **Catonsville** arose had been a portion of the property of the Baltimore Iron Works conveyed by Charles Carroll of

Carrollton to his eldest daughter Mary and her husband Richard Caton. A handsome young merchant newly arrived from Liverpool; Caton was not easily accepted by her father as suitable for the eldest daughter of the richest family in Maryland. Undoubtedly dependent on the Carroll connection, Caton dabbled in a variety of businesses when he became bankrupt in 1800 due to losses in a coal mining venture. From then on, he functioned as an agent of his long lived father-in-law. The latter remained generous in the support of his daughter and her family throughout their lives. Their extravagance was well known but also the success of their daughters' stellar marriages to the British nobility.

Situated on the relatively well built Frederick Turnpike, there was early subdivision of lots and some settlement even before the Civil War. Mount de Sales Academy run by the Sisters of Visitation was an early girl's school located at what would be Edmondson Avenue and the Beltway that attracted a national, even an international, student body. St Timothy's Hall was a military-style school that was the leading boy's preparatory school in the 1850s. Closed during the Civil War, it started up again and flourished until the 1870s. A number of fashionable homes were built in the 1870s with the advent of the street railway. Gas mains came to the town n 1885; water mains in 1886 by a local company that was absorbed by the Baltimore County Water and Electric Company in 1905. It was Baltimore County's most prosperous and settled town at the turn of the century.

Reistertown, at the intersection of the roads to Westminster and Hanover, grew as a stopping place a good day's journey from

Baltimore. Catering to travelers, there were hotels and taverns stretched along the roadway that is still a highly used commercial route. Emory Grove nearby was a Methodist campground and Glyndon an early resort development with a station on the Western Maryland Railroad on its way to and from the Hillon Street depot. Dr Harry Slade, whose name prominently remains as a street in Pikesville at the county line, came to Reistertown in the 1880s and remained the town physician for the next fifty years as well as health officer of Baltimore County.

Pikesville, named after the explorer Zebulon Pike, was a much smaller village. The Western Maryland Railroad extended to the northwest early with the local development of a station at Pikesville and to the flour mills at Owings Mills. A bastion of pro-Confederate sentiment, the great event of its Civil War history was the Confederate Johnson-Gilmor Raid of July 10-12 1864. It had a Federal Arsenal that became a Confederate Veterans Home. In 1889, Frederick Law Olmsted Sr designed "Sudbrook Village" as an early version of the suburb that would be replicated by his son and namesake later in the design of Roland Park. It still exists as an entity defined by a one lane bridge that crosses its brook.

Mount Washington was a station on the Northern Central Railroad to Harrisburg. Baltimore's first railroad suburb, it was first created as "Mount Washington Rural Retreat" solely for residential use in the 1850s to the west of a cotton factory village called Washingtonville dating from 1808. The Washington Cotton Manufacturing Company was the first in Maryland to be worked by water. After the death of the owner, the mill was bought in the 1850s by the owner of the far larger Clipper Mill in Woodberry.

Soon after, the estate of "Clover Hill" was bought to create a "suburban village" atop present day "Dixon Hill." Villa lots of 4 to 20 acres were offered with fronts "on wide avenues" on the west of was then still called the B&S Railroad. The goal was "to offer a healthy, retired and respectable country residence –having the conveniences of the city with the advantages of the country…at little less expense to ride downtown than to ride from Madison Avenue or Franklin Square."

Mount Washington Female College was founded, later in the 1860s and became the novitiate of the Sisters of Mercy whose Mount St Agnes College closed in 1971 after nearly seventy-five years. The original octagonal building is still intact atop the extensive cluster of more contemporary buildings now used as a Johns Hopkins Conference Center. The streetcar service starting in 1897 encouraged further development. Now once again, it is served by the Light Rail of the MTA.

The eastern part of Baltimore County would be industrial. In 1886, the Pennsylvania Steel Company decided to build a plant at tidewater to receive iron ore from abroad. The marshland at **Sparrows Point** was cheap; labor was readily available in East Baltimore and coal could be brought from West Virginia to produce steel in Bessemer furnaces. Slag from the furnaces served as landfill. A company town, one's residence reflected one's status. Management lived on A Street to C Street; white workers from D to H Streets;

blacks from I Street. The 20th century saw further industrial development of the eastern side of Baltimore County with the Glenn Martin plant along Middle River.

Ten thousand new units of housing were being built annually in the 1950s as former row house Baltimoreans and tenants sought a house of one's own with a lawn and its requisite power mower. The development of Towson as the county seat with its new county office building exemplified the increased significance of the county vis a vis the city. By the end of the 1950s, the population of Baltimore County exceeded one-half million; as that of Baltimore County rose; the city's share of the state's assessed wealth had fallen to one-third of the total from one-half a decade earlier. By the 1980s, the population of the county matched that of the city at about 750,000 each but with a far higher per capita income outside the city boundaries.

The Baltimore Beltway was the first of the interstate highways built under the Interstate Highway Act of 1956. It united the far flung portions of Baltimore County that had previously been reached only from and through the city. Already enjoying the boom in housing, commercial development now also occurred at the interchanges of the beltway. "Eastpoint" and "Westview" opened as regional shopping centers in the 1950s. With the completion of the highway, industry also moved where land was plentiful and cheap and trucks could more easily transport goods.

6.5. The Meyerhoff Family and Greater Baltimore

Joseph Meyerhoff was one of the leading builder-developers of the post-war era that helped create the present day regional nature of Baltimore. The story of the Meyerhoff family in Baltimore starts in 1906 at Locust Point when the seven year old Joseph arrived with his parents, the fifth of six children, refugees from the Russian pogroms of 1905. Their arrival nearly coincided with the gala celebrating Baltimore's recovery from the Great Fire of 1904.

Part of the Great Migration from the Jewish Pale of Settlement, the parents sold groceries and kosher meat where they lived in the 2300 block of Druid Hill Avenue just above North Avenue and the father worked as a part-time cantor. Growing up in what was then the Jewish neighborhood, he went the accelerated program at P.S. 49 that enabled him to enter college-bound Baltimore City College. Needing to work in the family store, he entered night school program at the University of Maryland Law School, finishing in 1920 after service in the army during World War I.

Fig. 47 - Joseph Meyerhoff

After practicing law, he entered the construction business with his brother selling lots at Glen Avenue east of Park Heights Avenue in what was then far off Northwest Baltimore. After his elder brother's bankruptcy in 1924, Meyerhoff paid off all the notes that were due but always remained aware in his future dealings of having experienced that difficulty. In the late 1920s and early 1930s, he built homes in the area of Northern Parkway near York Road and in Stoneleigh in Baltimore County, the latter in association with the Roland Park Company that maintained its restrictive racial policies.

Post-World War II, his company, called Monumental Properties reminiscent of the name given to Baltimore, built large tracts of houses and many shopping centers in the Baltimore region including a luxury apartment house Eleven Slade Avenue in Pikesville adjacent to the Baltimore Hebrew Congregation and the Jewish Suburban

Country Club where he himself lived. He also built houses and shopping centers elsewhere in the Middle Atlantic States as well as Georgia and Florida.

Meyerhoff remained heavily involved in Jewish charities and in the support of Israel. In light of the source of their wealth, the Meyerhoff family philanthropies in their mission statement continue "to invoke the Jewish tradition of 'tzedakah' in their pursuit of strengthening of the public and cultural organizations that support 'middle class' life in Baltimore and its region." The Meyerhoff family has continued to live within the Jewish community as that community migrated northwest as if a single unit along with its religious life into Baltimore County; into Pikesville and Owings Mills and beyond. By the end of the 1970s, two-thirds of a growing Jewish population had migrated from the city to elsewhere in the region.

Nevertheless, in the late 1940s when racial covenants were to be outlawed, the Baltimore Jewish Council found it was not possible to require Jewish developers such as Meyerhoff to renounce their business arrangements with the Roland Park Company, the most seriously discriminatory real estate company. In particular, Northwood was developed by Meyerhoff together with the Roland Park Company in accordance with their ongoing policies. However, the large number of smaller new developments in Baltimore County made such arrangements less viable. More recently, a more observant Jewish community has arisen close to the city border re-establishing families in the housing left behind by those who moved across the city line in search of better schools. There are newly built scattered smaller synagogues enabling congregants to walk to services.

After retirement from an active role in business, Joseph Meyerhoff devoted his energies to a number of activities, mainly to the building of the Baltimore Symphony Orchestra's first dedicated concert hall. It is now the centerpiece of the cultural district adjacent to the former Mt Royal B&O Station (now the Maryland Institute of Art) and the University of Baltimore campus. At the time of his death in 1985, his newspaper obituary particularly recognized him for that contribution to Baltimore; and described a memorial concert that reflected his tastes and a memorial service that filled the hall he helped create. The family has continued to endow buildings on the Goucher College campus as well as programs within the Baltimore Jewish community.

A descendant from a collateral branch derived from a younger brother of Joseph Meyerhoff, Robert Meyerhoff and his wife Jane created what is one of the world's largest collections of contemporary art. Housed at their horse farm in Hunt Valley, they chose to bequeath their collection not to the Baltimore Museum of Art as had the Cone sisters and the Adler sisters in the previous generation but to the National Gallery of Art based in Washington.

No sooner had the last streetcar closed its doors on its last passenger in the early 1960s, it became clear that a regional mass transit system would eventually be necessary. The U.S. Congress in 1964 passed the Urban Mass Transportation Act (UMTA) that provided federal funds for mass public transit. A "heavy rail" system was recommended following the traditional corridors: an in-town loop with six radii extending northwest, north, northeast and south, southeast and southwest. In 1970, the MTA (first the Metropolitan Transit Authority, later the Mass Transit Administration) took over the struggling bus lines of the Baltimore Transit Company (BTC).

With the in-town loop dropped aside from the eastern segment serving Johns Hopkins Hospital, the first line ran to the northwest eventually to Owings Mills following to the extent possible the tracks of the Western Maryland Railroad. The plan to follow the old Baltimore & Annapolis Railroad to the south to form a 28-mile subway was scrapped in 1975 when Anne Arundel County dropped out of the consortium. The active lobbying of Governor Mandel was necessary to proceed to any degree. All that remained was an eight-mile line to the northwest from Charles Center to Reistertown Plaza in 1983 to be finally supplemented to reach Owings Mills in 1987.

The tunneling extended four and a half miles from Charles Center though Bolton Hill (Upton Station) to Mondawin. It then rises at the former site of Carlin's Park (at Park Circle) aboveground before reaching West Cold Spring Lane on the way to Reistertown Plaza and beyond on a viaduct. The extension of the tunnel east to Johns Hopkins Hospital at Broadway was far more complex and costly. The low water table and the need to burrow through city streets precluded any further tunneling as a way to develop a regional transit system.

The northern line originally planned to Towson and Timonium was deferred; heavy rail was too costly to contemplate. The term "light-rail" is a misnomer; the weight of the cars does not differ.

Surface transportation rather than tunneling is one characteristic, overhead wires rather than third rail and minimal station facilities are the others. The presence of former Mayor William Donald Schaefer in the governor's chair in 1987 helped insure completion of the long-planned north-south line from Towson/Timonium (now extended to Hunt Valley) along the Northern Central Railroad right-of-way. The southern leg to Glen Burnie and the Baltimore/Washington International (BWI) Airport runs along the Baltimore & Annapolis Railroad right-of-way. The roadway of Howard Street is used for the downtown surface portion.

Based on its extensive use by low-cost Southwest Airlines, BWI has grown to become the busiest of the three airports in the Baltimore-Washington area. Opened in 1950, its name of Friendship Airport reflected the previous use of its site by a church of that name. Its name change to Baltimore-Washington International Airport in 1963 under the control of the Maryland State Department of Transportation reflected its projected regional reach. The connection to the AMTRAK and MARC railroad systems makes it particularly convenient to Washington while Dulles International Airport still until 2018 remains without rail connection to the District of Columbia.

So by April 1992, in a gesture to highlight its importance to the revitalization of Baltimore, the Light Rail System was inaugurated for the opening game at Oriole Park!

Fig. 48 - Baltimore Transit system

EPILOGUE

The problems of Baltimore are shared by many other large American cities in this post-industrial age. The "strangulation" of the City of Baltimore within its political boundaries with its loss of tax-paying population requires a regional "metropolitan" approach to the diffusion of the support of both the poor and the black throughout the entire area. The city and its region's commitment to the necessary solution apparently do not exist to the extent that has been required; they continue to struggle despite the extensive efforts made.

It is clearly still a city of "neighborhoods," where people identify themselves by their specific high school and neighborhood to which they feel drawn to return after time away. One man who had grown up in the Forest Park area recently returned after living in Washington and New York reminisces fondly of his elementary school years. Barry Levinson has mined his Baltimore memories for an entire series of his movies. When one young student from New York was asked why he planned to stay, his answer was "it's a homey place, yet big enough." It is an attractive place yet it remains disjointed in its search for solutions. One searches for the answers why it has been such a disjointed city.

Is it because it lies uneasily between the two sections of the country, the two cultures? A Southern city in its attitudes while also in the North, it has valued tradition to perhaps an excessive degree with its ruling white elite eager to move to the higher ground away from the city, reluctant to take action that might jeopardize their hegemony yet bring unity; subject to fits of violence that breeds the fear that arises in many conversations. A city of immigration of both blacks and whites, enclaves came about that were segregated by public policy, enshrined by short sighted narrow interests and fears of the other. The various immigrant groups, particularly the large second wave of Jews, were not easily welcomed to share power and contribute to the viability of the city by their German Jewish predecessors or the heavily church-going Christian ruling ethos. Now that the "immigrant Catholic Church" has mainly dissolved aided by Vatican II, no new more spiritual center yet holds. In the materialistic present, it is apparently only the sports teams that can cross boundaries.

Is the more intimate geography of the place also responsible for its divisiveness? An early amalgamation of three entities disrupted by the fall line rather than a unified city from the start, its streets do not come together to form a unified whole. Each time land was annexed to the city, the grid was superimposed to meet the needs of the land developers. The streets were laid out in local discrete segments. By developing each area separately, each such community safeguarded its boundaries and limited entry. The main streets run north-south to connect the central city and the suburbs. Due to its topography, there is much less availability of connection across town east west. The disunity was maintained that now characterizes its inhabitants not only in the city but also its region's relation with it.

Yet when visiting the city and meeting its people, one is struck by its energy, by the sheer grittiness of its people, by its surprisingly easy sharing in public spaces by both black and white, and by its parochial identity as a place where the "living is still easy."

THE END

TABLE OF FIGURES

Credit for maps to the Peabody Library of Johns Hopkins University. Credit for cover to Library of Congress map division.

BIBLIOGRAPHICAL ESSAY

There are a relatively large number of recent books about Baltimore that are oversized and heavily pictorial. The better of those are *Baltimore An Illustrated History* by Suanne Ellery Green Chapell (2000) and the far more substantial *Baltimore: The Building of an American City* by Sherry H. Olson. (1980, updated in 1997).*The Baltimore Book: New Views of Social History* (1991) explores in greater depth some of the social history not as recognized elsewhere. There are several books that explore both the streets and the architecture of the city such as *Streetwise Baltimore* by Carleton Jones (1990) and the excellent *Guide to Baltimore Architecture* by John Dorsey and James H. Dilts (3rd edition 1997) as well as *Walking in Baltimore: An Intimate Guide to the Old City* by Frank R. Shivers, Jr (1995). Very well done, eminently readable and relatively up-to-date but necessarily sketchy is the highly recommended *Charm City A Walk Through Baltimore* by Madison Smart Bell (2007) Michael Olesker's *Journeys to the Heart of Baltimore* (2001) is a very readable memoir that tells the story of the transition of the immigration generation into the American Baltimore; the story also told by Barry Levinson in several of his films. The neighborhoods of West and Northwest Baltimore are explored in a series of books by Roderick N. Ryon; one on North Baltimore by Karen Lewand, the last well equipped with maps; all published under the auspices of the University of Baltimore. John Waters' vision of Baltimore reveals it in its eccentricity and tawdriness; *The Wire* captures its violence and corruption. It still remains elusive.

There is a paucity of contemporary books dealing with the history of Maryland with any well-developed focus on the relationship between the city and the state. *Portrait of the Free State* by Donald M. Dozer (1982) is dated in its approach. *Baltimore on the Chesapeake* by Hamilton Owens (1941), although old and limited in its scope does attempt to be incisive. The most recent but still not up-to-date *Maryland: Middle Temperment* by Robert Brugger (1988) is a very large book that attempts to be comprehensive up to the 1980s but in so doing, is far less incisive. George H. Calcott's *Maryland and America 1940-1980 (*1985*)* is readable and inclusive particularly in its handling of the civil rights movement but relatively superficial in its treatment of the relationship between the city, county and state. Particularly recommended in its exploration of the different parts of the state is *Slavery and Freedom on the Middle Ground* by Barbara J. Fields (1985).

WORKS CONSULTED

Adler, Susan Helen. Saidie May.Pioneer of Early 20th Century Painting. Privately printed, 2008.

Basalik, Kenneth J. Urban Development in the Eastern United States: An Archeological View of Baltimore, Maryland. Ph.D.Dissertation, Temple University, 1994.

Beirne, Francis F. The Amiable Baltimoreans. Baltimore: Johns Hopkins University Press 1951.

Beirne, Francis F. and Carleton Jones. Baltimore: A Pictorial History. Baltimore, MD: The Maryland Historical Society, 1982.

Bell, Madison S. Charm City. A Walk through Baltimore. New York: Crown Publishers, 2007

Brooks, Neal A. and Eric G. Rockel. A History of Baltimore County. Towson, MD, 1979.

Brugger, Robert J. Maryland. A Middle Temperment. Baltimore: Johns Hopkins University Press, 1988.

Callcott, George H. Maryland and America 1940-1980. Baltimore: Johns Hopkins University Press, 1985

Catton, William B. John W. Garrett and the Baltimore & Ohio: A Study in Seaport and Railroad Competition. Doctoral Dissertation Northwestern University 1959.

Chapelle, Suzanne. Baltimore: An Illustrated History. Sun Valley, CA: American Historical Press, 2000.

Dilts, James. D. The Great Road. The Building of the Baltimore and Ohio, the Nation's First Railroad, 1828-1853. Stanford: Stanford University Press, 1993

Dorsey, John and James D. Dilts. A Guide to Baltimore Architecture. Centreville, MD: Tidewater Publishers, 1997.

Dozer, Donald M. Portrait of the Free State. Cambridge, MD: Tidewater Publishers, 1976.

Douglas, George H. H.L. Mencken. Critic of American Life. Archon Books: Hampden Connecticut, 1978.

Douglass, Frederick. My Bondage and My Freedom. New York: Dover Publications, 1969.

Elfenbein, Jessica, Thomas L. Hollowak, and Elizabeth M. Nix. Baltimore'68 Riots and Rebirth in an American City. Philadelphia: Temple University Press, 2011.

Farrell, Michael R. The History if Baltimore's Streetcars. Sykeville, MD: Greenberg Publishing Company, 1992.

Fee, Elizabeth, Linda Shopes and Linda Zeidman. The Baltimore Book. New Views of Local History. Philadelphia: Temple University Press, 1991.

Fein, Isaac. The Making of an American Jewish Community. Philadelphia: Jewish Publication Society, 1971.

Fields, Barbara J. Slavery and Freedom on the Middle Ground. New Haven: Yale University Press, 1985.

Garitee, Jerome. The Republic's Private Navy. Mystic CN: Mystic Seaport Press, 1977.

Gibson, Larry. Young Thurgood. Amherst New York: Prometheus Books, 2012.

Glassmire, Karilyn A. Baltimore: Port of Entry. Master Dissertation University of Maryland, 2008.

Gunz, Dieter. The Maryland Germans. Port Washington NY: The Kennikat Press, 1948.

Hayward, Mary E. and Charles Belfoure. The Baltimore Row House. New York: Princeton Architectural Press, 1999.

Hickey, Donald R. The War of 1812. A Forgotten Conflict. Urbana: University of Illinois Press, 2012.

Hidy, Muriel. George Peabody, Merchant and Financier. New York: Arno Press, 1974.

Hoffman, Ronald. Princes of Ireland, Planters of Maryland. A Carroll Saga 1500-1782. Chapel Hill: University of North Carolina Press, 2000.

Holcombe, Eric L. The City as Suburb. A History of Northeast Baltimore. Chicago: Columbia College, 2008

Hungerford, Edward. The Story of the Baltimore and Ohio Railroad 1827-1927. New York: Arno Press, 1973.

Johnson, Gerald W. et al. The *Sunpapers* of Baltimore. New York: Alfred A Knopf, 1937.

Jones, Carleton. Streetwise Baltimore. Chicago: Bonus Books, 1990.

Krugler, John D. English and Catholic. The Lords Baltimore in the Seventeenth Century. Baltimore: Johns Hopkins University Press, 2004.

Lieb, Emily. Row House City: Unbuilding Baltimore 1940-1980. Doctoral Dissertation, Columbia University, 2010.

Nast, Lenora, Laurence N. Krauss and R.C. Monk. Baltimore: A Living Renaissance. Baltimore: Historic Baltimore Society, 1982.

Olson, Sherry. Baltimore Imitates the Spider. Annals of the Association of American Geographers. v. 69 (Dec 1979) pp 557-574.

Olson, Sherry. Baltimore: The Building of an American City. Baltimore: Johns Hopkins University Press, 1997.

Owens, Hamilton. Baltimore on the Chesapeake. Garden City, NY: Doubleday, Doran & Company, Inc., 1941.

Pancake, John. Samuel Smith and the Politics of Business 1752-1839. Tuscaloosa: University of Alabama Press, 1972.

Parker, Franklin. George Peabody. Nashville: Vanderbilt University Press, 1995.

Pietila, Antero. Not in my Neighborhood. Chicago: Ivan R. Dee, 2010.

Richardson, Brenda. Dr Claribel and Miss Etta. The Cone Collection. Baltimore: The Baltimore Museum of Art, n.d.

Rockman, Seth. Scraping By. Baltimore: Johns Hopkins University Press, 2009.

Rusk, David. Baltimore Unbound. Baltimore: Johns Hopkins University Press/Abell Foundation, 1996.

Scharf, J. Thomas. The Chronicles of Baltimore. Bowie, MD: Heritage Books, 1989. (Facsimile of 1874 edition)

Shrivers, Frank R. Jr. Walking in Baltimore: An Intimate Guide to the Old City. Baltimore: Johns Hopkins University Press, 1995.

Skaggs, David C. The Roots of Maryland Democracy. 1753-1776. Westport CN: The Greenwood Press, 1973.

Spaulding, Thomas W. The Premier See. A History of the Baltimore Archdiocese. Baltimore: Johns Hopkins University Press. 1989.

Stover, John F. The History of the Baltimore and Ohio Railroad. West Lafayette: University of Purdue Press, 1987

Travers, Paul J. The Patapsco. Baltimore's River of History. Centreville, MD: Maryland Historical Society, 1990.

Witcover, Jules White Knight. The Rise of Spiro Agnew. New York: Random House, 1972.

INDEX

ABOUT THE AUTHOR

Mark N. Ozer, in his travels and lectures, has explored the interaction of history and geography of many of the great cities of the world. A resident of Washington since 1964, he has written about its unique history as the national capital. Baltimore has been during those years a city for which he has had a close personal affinity and has had ongoing interest as a great American city so different from its close neighbor. See markozerbooks.com.

Made in the USA
Middletown, DE
20 October 2015